"This is an amazing and intriguing account of how a young, 16-year-old boy from a middle-class family in India made the life-changing decision to go to America. Mr. Jesudian holds one's attention captive as he works through the various challenges he faced, from his visa application until stepping aboard the airplane destined for New York City. Once you read this book, you will clearly understand how America has been enriched by many immigrants from around the world. However, this book is much more than just a 'success story.' It assimilates the values of a God-centered life, perseverance, determination, struggle, victory, and critical analysis of available options. Inside the book, Mr. Jesudian develops his 'God Principle' and the importance then of implementation. With this solid foundation, he explores the different forms of government and details his reasoning for choosing America. He concludes with nonnegotiable principles we must adhere to in order to succeed in a free society.

You will find this book refreshing, captivating, and hard to put down!"

—**Vice Admiral Toney Michael Bucchi**,
Vice Admiral US Navy Retd.

"Leo Jesudian's autobiography reads like an entrepreneur's how-to book. It also tells the story of a fascinating individual."

—**Dr. Daniel Pipes**,
President Middle East Forum

"Riveting and insightful! I love this real-life true story. Thank you, Leo, for opening up your heart and imparting such valuable life lessons to us. Do yourself a favor; find a quiet place and get ready for the adventure that awaits you."

—**Rev. Jonathan DelTurco**,
Founder and Lead Pastor,
International Family Church

"I have known Leo for over 50 years. He was a smart, intelligent teenager who, even at that young age, could discuss varied subjects with clarity and confidence and had a vision of his ambitious future. So when he sent me his book *Hard Work and the American Dream*, I was thrilled and more than pleased. I read the book in one sitting as it was too good to put down. His anecdotes of his plights and success were interesting and encouraging.

Son and grandson of an Army upbringing, Leo had a disciplined life and developed self-confidence and determination early on. In his inspiring, concise memoir, he has depicted his plight superbly and fulfilled his ambitions with conviction and hard work. Life in America was not easy for him, but he knew that with determination, he would win 'to get his dreams fulfilled.'

The book will be a source of inspiration and encouragement to all young aspirants who like to dream big and are ready to face challenges in life. I have thoroughly enjoyed reading the book and am sure you will enjoy it, too."

—**Wing Commander Dr. K. L. Sindhi**,
Retd. Veteran,
Indian Air Force

"Leo Jesudian is one of the most unique people I have had the privilege of knowing. He is brilliant, perceptive, and inspirational. Leo's life story is amazing and is the foundation from which he analyzes the world. *Hard Work and the American Dream* will renew your belief in America's democracy, stir your faith in God, and inspire you to accomplish your dreams!"

—**Wendy Tatro**,
International Director,
Living Word Missions

HARD WORK AND THE AMERICAN DREAM
AN IMMIGRANT STORY

LEO D. JESUDIAN

CLAY BRIDGES
PRESS

Hard Work and the American Dream
An Immigrant Story

Copyright © 2021 by Leo D. Jesudian

Published by Clay Bridges in Houston, TX

www.claybridgespress.com

All rights reserved. No part of this publication may be reproduced, stored in a retrieval system, or transmitted in any form by any means, electronic, mechanical, photocopy, recording, or otherwise, without the prior permission of the publisher, except as provided for by USA copyright law.

ISBN 978-1-953300-39-3 (paperback)
ISBN 978-1-953300-40-9 (hardback)
ISBN 978-1-953300-41-6 (ebook)

Special Sales: Most Clay Bridges titles are available in special quantity discounts. Custom imprinting or excerpting can also be done to fit special needs. For standard bulk orders, go to www.claybridgesbulk.com. For specialty press or large orders, contact Clay Bridges at info@claybridgespress.com.

I dedicate this book to Tiffany, my beautiful wife of 34 years. She has been by my side during the extreme ups and downs I have gone through. She literally wakes up every morning with a huge smile that is very contagious. Tiffany, my world is amazingly better because of you. Thank you for who you are and what you stand for. I am blessed to have you as my wonderful wife, my fabulous friend, my beautiful and brainy business partner, and my comfortable, caring confidant.

TABLE OF CONTENTS

CHAPTER 1
The Challenge of Getting an American Visa   1

CHAPTER 2
Arguing My Case   9

CHAPTER 3
What Makes Me Tick   19

CHAPTER 4
An Abbreviated History of My Childhood
through College   29

CHAPTER 5
Decision to Visit the USA   35

CHAPTER 6
Why America?   39

CHAPTER 7
Acquiring the Finances to Achieve My Dream   65

CHAPTER 8
A Decision to Abort Further Studies   73

CHAPTER 9 Leading Up to Leaving India	85
CHAPTER 10 Becoming Unrelatable in My Community	89
CHAPTER 11 The Deal That Started It All	97
CHAPTER 12 New York, New York	105
CHAPTER 13 Move to Boston	119
CHAPTER 14 God's Work in a Nutshell	125
CHAPTER 15 Preparing to Leave for India	127
CHAPTER 16 The Trip to India	133
CHAPTER 17 Back in the USA	141
CHAPTER 18 A Financial Landslide	145
CHAPTER 19 Always Looking to Grow	155
CHAPTER 20 Store Number Two on the Cape	159
CHAPTER 21 Store Number Three in Back Bay	165

CHAPTER 22
Parents' Maiden Visit to the USA   173

CHAPTER 23
Store Number Four in Newport, Rhode Island   189

CHAPTER 24
First Foray into Importing from Mexico   191

CHAPTER 25
Importing from Afghanistan   197

CHAPTER 26
Diversifying More   205

CHAPTER 27
Success Is Sweet Revenge   237

Chapter 1

THE CHALLENGE OF GETTING AN AMERICAN VISA

It was winter in New Delhi. The temperature during the day was in the mid 50s to low 60s Fahrenheit, while at night it dropped to the mid 30s to low 40s. People wore sweaters, shawls, hats, and woolen scarves (called mufflers) and complained about a cold snap caused by the snowfall in Darjeeling. It was November 30, 1970. I was staying at my sister and brother-in-law's house on an air base on the outskirts of New Delhi. My brother-in-law was a Squadron Leader (Major) in the Indian Air Force. He was second in command at 25 Wing—one of two Air Force missile defense installations guarding the capital city of New Delhi. It was my nephew's (the younger of their two sons) birthday. On that memorable day, my nephew turned one. I was super excited for two reasons: (1) it was my nephew's birthday, and (2) it happened to be the day I was going to the US Embassy in New Delhi to get a tourist visa so I could visit the United States of America.

Since my sister and brother-in-law were living on the outskirts of New Delhi, it was convenient for me to stay with them while I got my plan in motion to visit the United States. I was told that I needed to get a round trip ticket to the United States and have a valid passport in hand before I could go to the US Embassy to apply for and get a tourist visa. Simple? I learned another very important lesson in life. The opposite of simple is complex. The opposite of easy is hard. Simple and complex have to do with understanding. Easy and hard have to do with doing. Something very simple to comprehend can be extremely hard to do. The first and one of the most monumentally hard things I have ever achieved in my life was getting a visa from the US Embassy in New Delhi to visit the United States.

According to Indian standards of income and living expenses, I paid a huge amount of money to buy a round trip ticket to New York. I was nervous and excited all at once. However, I was fired up about visiting America, which gave me the guts and the gall, along with the audacity and the chutzpah, to spend the inordinate amount of money required to buy that round trip ticket to the USA and have the additional money to stay in the United States for as long as I planned.

My father, a career army officer, had taken leave from

THE CHALLENGE OF GETTING AN AMERICAN VISA

his base to come to New Delhi with my mom to give me a send-off. Mom and Dad arrived in New Delhi a few days before I was ready to get my visa. I borrowed my brother-in-law's car to go to the US Embassy. My mother and I left at 8:00 a.m. on November 30, 1970, armed with a round trip ticket to New York City and a valid passport, to drive to the US Embassy to get me a visa. I was not intellectually devoid, but boy, was I naïve! We arrived at the embassy a few minutes before 9:00 a.m. and saw a line of 75 to 100 people already in place. For some dumb reason, I thought I was going to saunter into the embassy alone and sit in a comfortable chair until I was called to submit my application. Not so.

After I stood in line for about 30 minutes, the group was ushered through a gate where armed US Marines were all over the place. I was not uncomfortable with that since I had grown up on a military base and was used to armed guards and MPs everywhere. I was not at all surprised at the security. We were all given applications and asked to take a seat in a large hall and fill out the forms to the best of our abilities. Then we were told to go to Window #4 and submit our applications. We were further informed that our visas, if approved, would be ready after lunch and we should return at 1:30 p.m. I was a bit concerned about the language "if approved," but I dismissed it. I was confident that I would certainly be approved.

I went out jauntily, and my mother—who happened to be the most ardent prayer warrior I had ever known—was sitting in the passenger seat of the car, eyes shut tight, hands folded, praying for me. I tapped on the window. She said with a big smile, "So you got your visa?" Getting into the car, I said, "No, we have to come back after lunch and pick it up." So we both decided to go to Connaught Place, a very upscale shopping area in New Delhi, spend some time looking around, have lunch, and then return to pick up my visa.

At 1:30 p.m., I stood in line again for about another 30 minutes, and then the group was escorted inside again. We were told that when our name was called in alphabetical order, we should go to Window #3 to get the results of our applications. I was in the first half of the group because my last name started with J. When my name was called, I excitedly walked up to Window #3 to get my visa. To my surprise, a huge red word—DENIED—was stamped diagonally across my application. My heart sank. I felt weak as though someone had clocked me square in my face with a sledgehammer.

I looked at the application and for a split second was at a loss for words. Then I sputtered out aloud, "What's this?"

The man behind Window #3 said, "What does it look like, kid? You have been denied."

I was incensed and blurted out, "Why?"

The man said, "You don't have the right to ask why. You just accept what the US Embassy decides."

I suddenly got hold of myself, calmly looked him in the eye, and said, "I want to speak to your superior."

He laughed out loud and said, "Kid, you have no choice but to accept the verdict."

THE CHALLENGE OF GETTING AN AMERICAN VISA

"Verdicts are rendered in a court of law. I just applied for a visa, for Pete's sake."

Because of this rather loud banter, another man from behind the counter came to the window and said, "What's going on?" With a big smile, the first man behind Window #3 explained my ridiculous demand. The other man dismissively said, "Give the guy an appeal form."

I was shocked at the words he used—*verdict, appeal*—as if I had done something wrong and was being prosecuted. It was as though I had lost a legal case and was being allowed to appeal the verdict when all I had done was apply for a freaking visa. I took the appeal form and filled it out. I handed it to the man behind Window #3. After looking it over, the man said, "Come back tomorrow, kid. This application now goes all the way up to the Consul General who will review your case."

I am thinking that now that I have a verdict, I am going to appeal my case.

The man went on to say, "The Consul General will have an answer for you tomorrow." Then he said, "Oh! By the way, in the two years I have been here, I have never had anyone appeal a denied verdict, so I wouldn't get my hopes up, kid. Good luck!"

I went to the car with a hangdog expression on my face, and of course, my mother was again deep in prayer for me. I got into the car and startled her. She said excitedly, "Do you get your visa? Let me see it."

I said I was denied, and she said, "Why?"

I said, "Exactly. *Why?*"

We went home, discussing things that didn't make

much sense at all. I am usually a happy, aggressive, fun-loving person. My spirits were down like never before. I knew I needed to get hold of myself and get ready for an uphill battle. I certainly didn't have a clue for how to engage in this kind of battle, but I was acutely aware of the fact that I had a huge battle on my hands. All of a sudden, something very simple and straightforward to understand became a very hard thing to do.

This now became a monumental task, and I didn't have plan B. My mother assured me that the US Embassy was no match for God and that because she was praying, they would have to give me my visa. I wanted so badly to believe her, but I dare say I was not that willing in the belief department yet. You see, God wants to prove what he can do for you if only you have the belief of a mustard seed. Due to that miniscule belief, he will arm you with the courage you need to engage in the battle required of you to win. I definitely had the belief of a mustard seed, and hence I was given the will to engage.

The next day, I arrived at the Embassy and went right in since there was no line. I put two and two together and deduced that the US Embassy did not take visa applications every day. I sat and waited tentatively, not knowing how things were going to go. Though I had thought about it almost all night, I didn't have a clue of what was going to transpire. The Marines stood on duty at ease, motionless and seemingly emotionless, looking straight forward. People were busy at their desks. After what seemed like an inordinate amount of time (it really was maybe only 20 minutes), I was approached by a

THE CHALLENGE OF GETTING AN AMERICAN VISA

smart, tall, lean, athletically built woman in an Air Force uniform with a rank on her epaulets, not on her sleeve. That meant she was an officer. I later found out that she was a Major. She was very sharp and erect in her stature. With a hint of a smile, which was such a breath of fresh air, she said, "Mr. Jesudian?" She pronounced my name perfectly and didn't call me kid. She called me Mister.

I said, "Yes?"

"Follow me, Sir. Consul General Thomas will see you now."

I felt proud and nervous all at the same time and did all I could to control my excitement. I was going to be seen by the Consul General—the number-two person in the US Embassy, just below the Ambassador. I followed the Major down a wall-to-wall carpeted hallway that was washed in white fluorescent light. She knocked briefly with a strong rap on a door to the left. A muffled voice said, "Come in." Not quite entering the room, she opened the door wide and announced in a firm but very pleasant voice, "Consul General, Sir. Mr. Jesudian here to see you."

As I walked in, I heard the door close. The Consul General and I were alone in this vast room. His office was huge and intimidating. He sat behind a formidable, shiny, solid, oversized mahogany desk with a huge American flag to his right, which was to my left. On the wall was a large picture of Richard M. Nixon with a brass plate at the bottom that read, "Richard M. Nixon, President of the United States of America." To the left of the Consul General's desk was an oversized, shiny, brass

American eagle mounted on a 7-foot, ultra-polished brass pole. It was very intimidating to a 19-year-old. The Consul General knew that and may have even relished the process of so-called lesser humans coming into his high office. Also on the wall was a plaque stating that the Consul General was a US Attorney. We called attorneys barristers or solicitors (a title for a lawyer left over from the British colonial days), but I knew what an attorney was. Being naïve, I didn't know why he made it a point to print US in front of the word *Attorney*—that was a given, right? He was an American, and he was an attorney. So naturally, he was a US attorney. Well, I learned much later on what it really meant to be a US Attorney. The Consul General got up, shook my hand, and asked me to take a seat. After getting over the initial anger of the huge red DENIED stamp on my application and the casual way the man at Window #3 kept calling me kid (which I found to be a mild put-down), I was taken up with the genuine dignity of the environment I was in.

Chapter 2

ARGUING MY CASE

Consul General Thomas started the conversation by saying, "Mr. Jesudian, I genuinely understand your desire to visit the USA. You know, we have a very amazing country, and everyone, their sons and daughters around the world, want to live in the USA. That being said, you will have to take the time to convince me that your intentions to visit the United States of America are truly that."

I looked at him, perplexed, and said, "What makes you, Sir, for one moment think that my intentions are untrue? I take umbrage to the fact that you imply that I am a liar. I have not broken any law, and I was advised that I have a case against me. I was also told that I have been delivered a one-sided verdict as I was not party to the process that delivered this verdict. So I am, as we speak, in the process of an appeal. Sir, all I am guilty of is applying for a visa to visit the USA."

Then he gave me a quick lesson in legal and politically correct language, and I heard a word I had never heard before. He said, "Oh! I don't mean to imply that you lie at all. However, we at all our consulates are well aware of the mistruths [that was the word I had never heard before] being uttered by individuals who want visas to enter the USA."

"Well," I said, "I am not one of those so-called individuals you refer to that utter mistruths, which is really a euphemism for a lie, Sir. How does applying for a visa get mistaken for a mistruth by someone as esteemed as yourself? I just want to visit America." I further said, "Sir, I value myself and have never been devious, especially if it is for no rhyme or reason. I have no reason to lie to you. I have bought a round trip ticket at a great personal expense to visit America, and that is exactly what I intend to do."

"Ah!" he said. "But you do have a reason to utter a mistruth. You see, everyone wants to visit the USA; however, they omit the fact that their true intention is to immigrate and not to visit. They go and don't come back. They use the visa to gain entry into the country, and once there, they either abscond and go underground, get admission in a college, illegally get married, and feign a desire to live with their so-called spouse, or apply for refugee status and tie up our legal system. You, Mr. Jesudian, must convince me that you will not do any of the things I mentioned and will, in fact, come back to

India, or I will not reverse my decision to not grant you a visa to visit America."

"I cannot make a commitment about the future," I said. "We all know we can plan all we want, and sometimes the future has a tendency to take us in a whole new direction. I can say one thing for sure. I am sincere in my desire to visit America and return. I have a round trip ticket. What if, in fact, I like the USA so much that I would like to stay? Is it not possible for me to legally get permission to do so?"

"Aha!" the Consul General said. "Mr. Jesudian, it did not take long for me to get to the bottom of it. I am more convinced now than when you walked in that you will indeed not return from the US once you are granted a visa. Moreover, everybody who visits the US loves it and wants to stay. So you just might have lost your case, young man."

"Sir," I replied, let me understand you clearly. You are unequivocally stating that my being honest with you is going to cost me a desire that I have had to visit the USA since I was five years old. Is that correct?"

He jumped in and said, "What desire does a five-year old boy born in India have about going to America?" He shrugged, rolled his eyes and hissed, "Please!"

"I was five years old when my grandfather told me that if ever I got a chance, I should visit America. He was not just mouthing off what he thought was a great place to visit. He just happened to be the first Indian from India to graduate from an American university Phi Beta Kapa with a PhD in English literature. He went to

Rutgers University on the banks of the Raritan in New Jersey."

The Consul General immediately looked me in the eye and knew I was not lying. At that time—1970—he would be hard pressed to find a 19-year-old anywhere in India who would know what a Phi Beta Kappa key was, and neither would that very same 19-year-old know that Rutgers University was situated on the banks of the Raritan River in New Jersey. Remember, it was 1970. These details were not common knowledge. This exchange got me a reprieve in my case. He had a faint smile, and I knew I had scored. He also understood that I was an intelligent, articulate young man and was obviously intrigued by my demeanor and ability to go toe-to-toe with him verbally. Remember, he was a US Attorney who was used to representing the United States government in criminal trials. He thrived on good argument.

He still seemed to want to grill me, though. He said, "You are young, unattached, and therefore a prime candidate to not come back. Though you speak very well for a young Indian man, I am not yet convinced. Mr. Jesudian, I have a very busy schedule. I have matters to attend to. I will let you further argue and grant you a chance to plead your case. I am going to ask you to come back tomorrow at 9:00 a.m., and we will pick up where we left off." He got up and said, "Good day!"

I had so much to say, but I held back and said, "Good day," shook his hand, and walked out of his office. I felt good that I was coming back, but I was not ecstatic because I had not accomplished my goal to get a visa.

ARGUING MY CASE

I approached the car and saw my mother praying. I opened the door, and she said, "What happened?" I told her, and she was very proud. I told her that every time I thought I was getting ahead and reaching him, he kept repeating that I had not convinced him yet.

"I want to ask you something, Son," my mother said. "How did you come up with the back-and-forth argument so easily with him? Did you think things through yesterday?"

"No," I said. "I have never been through anything like this. How on earth can I prepare to debate this guy when I know nothing about the issue and the thoughts going through his mind? In fact, I did not even know what we were going to talk about. Mom, this was really beyond me."

She smiled wide and said, "I knew it! I prayed all the while I was in the car that God would put words in your mouth to counteract the words of the Consul General, just like he did for Moses when he went before Pharaoh in Egypt to obtain the release of the Hebrews from their bondage."

I thought about that, and I was in awe. It was true. Without knowing it, I was going toe-to-toe with a US Attorney, the Consul General of the US Embassy in New Delhi. Theoretically, I was the most inept, unqualified adversary with zero background or legal stature to argue my case against a seasoned attorney who had tons of experience representing and arguing cases for the United States government. However, I seemed to hold my own very easily. None of that fluid argument was rehearsed; it was God who gave me the words I needed to argue with the Consul General. Wow! In a brief moment of levity, I asked my mom if she could pray to God to deliver some plagues to my adversary. We both laughed.

I got to the Embassy the next morning, and now the staff was saying hello and smiling, and the mood was very upbeat. They knew me now since it was my third visit. It was very intriguing to them that the Consul General was giving me a repeated audience. I later learned they were experiencing something unprecedented and hence their seemingly pro behavior toward me. They were witnessing a Rocky story unfolding in front of their eyes—the underdog showing some nerve.

I was ushered in by the same smart Major. I entered the Consul General's office. He toyed with me for about an hour and again said he was busy and that I should come back after lunch at 2:00 p.m. I went outside to my mom and said I felt like he was living through a vicarious thrill because he was playing with me and my emotions. He knows he is far superior to me in intellect, stature, experience, and power. She said, "Stop behaving ungratefully. I am praying, and God will break him down. As long as he is willing to see you, you will keep going there, and God will do the rest."

The Consul General again toyed with me, sometimes behaving like he believed me and other times telling me he was not convinced at all. This was going on and on. One time I entered his office, totally frustrated, and asked him, "Why don't you take down all those huge, hypocritical, four-color glossy posters that say Visit Los

ARGUING MY CASE

Angeles, Visit Miami, Visit New York City when all you are about is teasing people and wielding your power to inhibit them from visiting these so-called wonderful places?" He was stunned at my tirade and had no answer.

Over the next week, I went to the Consul General's office nine times, sometimes in the morning and sometimes in the afternoon. Every time I went home, it was awful. The environment at home was morose. This Consul General Thomas was affecting our whole family, not just me. We were a very happy family, but now, everyone was quiet and spoke in undertones as if we were going to disturb someone.

The Embassy staff had never seen anything like this. They were genuinely flabbergasted that I was not given a one-way ticket out of there to anywhere. They knew the Consul General to be an extremely busy man, yet he kept wanting to meet with me. They were completely nonplussed about the banter they were not privy to.

On the 10th trip, I was angry. My mother yelled at me and told me to stop having a bad attitude and behaving in an immature manner. She said, "Keep talking to him." I wanted to end the ordeal. I was escorted to the Consul General's office by my buddy, the very sharp and oh so courteous female officer, the Major who never spoke to me much other than the basic salutation and minimal discourse. Yet I felt she respected me for holding my own with the Consul General. She had a very nice attitude toward me. For that reason, I considered her my buddy.

I walked into the Consul General's office, sat down without being asked to sit, and lit a cigarette—the height of disrespect. Without lifting his head, the Consul General tersely said, "Put that cigarette out." I did immediately. He looked up and asked, "Can I help you?" I was about to respond with amazement when he said (with his hands in the air to stop me from talking), "Mr. Jesudian." With a big smile, he continued. "I have approved your visa for the United States of America. You can go to Window #2 and get your passport stamped."

Exhilarated, I ran around his enormous desk as he stood up and stepped back, perplexed. I hugged him and thanked him, mumbling and repeating my thank yous profusely. He did not hug me back; he did not know how. He just stood there, a stoic gentleman with his hands hanging limply by his side. He awkwardly wished me well, and we shook hands. I didn't walk out of his office; I floated out of his office. The staff applauded when I got to the outer office to get my visa at Window #2. Obviously, they all knew I had finally been approved. I had achieved the impossible, according to them. Quietly, they were actually rooting for me.

What had transpired was due to my mother's pure belief and her unceasing intercessory prayers. God put words in my mouth. Hence, the Consul General of the US Embassy in New Delhi in 1970 did not stand a chance from the very beginning. He had to acquiesce, and just like Pharaoh, he finally relented and gave in. God—not me—through the prayers of a huge believer (my mother) and through the mouth of her 19-year-old son, obliterated a US Attorney in an argument that lasted days. I won, with God's help!

It is hilarious what young, legal immigrants say to me all the time when they know how long I have been in the USA. They make this statement almost verbatim with gusto: "It was fairly easy for you to get a visa in those days; it is very difficult now." I smile and listen to their stories of woe. Most come here to study or have been offered a job. They never get turned down unless they are criminals. The most they had to do was comply with some documentation, which might have delayed them some. They don't have a clue how difficult it was for me to get a visa. What is it about humans who think their challenges are the most difficult and that no one else understands their predicaments? Life is tough, and only the strong-willed, focused, disciplined, and persevering humans excel. The rest live mediocre lives or even less.

Chapter 3

WHAT MAKES ME TICK

I am going to backtrack and give you a little insight so you can better comprehend what motivated me as a young man to make a key decision that was not only momentous but hugely impactful in my life. This is not a religious book, but it is definitely a book about the perseverance, stick-to-itiveness, focus, and discipline of a very Christian individual. I am certain that none of what I have accomplished in my life would have been possible if I didn't give all the glory to God the all-powerful who brings to fruition all good things.

For those who believe or are open-minded, you will get some deep insights into how God orchestrates things to fall into place in order for an individual's dreams to be realized. Without a shadow of a doubt, God's orchestration never exempts anyone from the work ethic required, the focus involved, and the persistence needed to achieve that dream. No one, no matter how talented they may be, can achieve any victory without a struggle. Victory always follows struggle. It is never the other way around. Sometimes the struggle might be physical; other times it could be mental, emotional, or oftentimes financial. I have been through a combination of struggles that makes the victory all the more succulent. The larger the dream, the more seemingly insurmountable is the struggle. Nothing is insurmountable, but so many things seem to be. Satan makes sure everyone thinks things are insurmountable. It is up to us to deny Satan that power of influence and align ourselves with God. Here is the common denominator: Things should be done right.

Easy things deliver low returns, and hard things deliver high returns. My advice to everyone is this: Choose hard things so you always make a high return on your efforts. Never wimp out and take the easy road. It guarantees mediocrity or less. No matter what, struggle you must in order to enjoy any victory. When God's orchestration in our lives is properly understood, the results are extremely poignant. You will find that I interlace my blessings from God throughout this book. Don't be offended if you are an atheist or an agnostic. I trust you will still consider this a good read anyway. Why? Because 85 percent of all I write about is true and has actually transpired. So what about the 15 percent? I kept no journal since I worked all waking hours of the day. This book is all from memory—a very vivid memory, I might add. I also have changed the names of the real people in this book to keep their identities confidential. In some places, I must admit, I have embellished some things so they sound more impactful. When someone tells you a story and then they don't get the desired response, they say, "You had to have been there." I never want that to be the case, so I write in a manner to negate that emotion of, "You had to have been there."

There was no way that I—a young, first-year (freshman) student attending college in India, the son of an army officer—could afford to visit the USA. You will be well within your rights to ask why.

This is why.

In December 1970, that round-trip airline ticket I bought from New Delhi to New York and back cost roughly what a newly commissioned Indian Air Force MIG 21 fighter pilot earned in eight months. And in those days, a round trip ticket was valid for a whole year with the travel dates wide open. So how did a teenager come up with that kind of money, not to mention the cash I needed over and above that amount to be able to live in the USA for however long I was going to stay there as a tourist?

This is one of the segments where, if you are a believer, you will comprehend how God works. At this point, people who do not believe in God say, "You are unnecessarily bringing God into the equation when it is just your hard work, persistence, and being at the right place at the right time that brought you the success you have." I laugh and say, "I have an ego the size of Texas. If I could take 100 percent of the credit for all the things I have done and accomplished, believe you me, I would.

Why should I give credit to God if I did it all myself?" Think about it. In fact, my input in the equation was this: "I worked hard, I worked smart, I persevered, and I believed. The fruits of my work and belief were all God!"

My mother read the Bible every day. She was the only person I know who read it cover-to-cover repeatedly until she died. She taught me to do the same, and I have done it and am doing it. I have lost count of how many times I have read the Bible cover-to-cover. From a historic point of view, it is the most profound piece of literature, poetry, intrigue, violence, and mystery I have ever read. It is also the most profound handbook to resolve all issues humankind will ever face—a guide, if you will. Nonbelievers say, "The Bible could never be the word of God. It was written by old men." Well, how is this for something confounding?

Over millennia, scores of diverse writers (old men, if you insist) have threaded a continuous story that is brought to a head with a prediction by the prophet Isaiah about Jesus Christ being born, more than 600 years prior to Jesus's being incarnate. How is that explained as human work? Humans cannot even agree on a simple task to be done in a board room, never mind agreeing to write a fake narrative over millennia. Due to my deep understanding of this amazing book, I justly give God all the glory for any and all my accomplishments. I take responsibility for my actions based on the choices I make and nothing else. My choices are a God-given right for me to exercise free will. Through the pages of this book, hopefully you, the reader, will further understand where

I am coming from. Everything that transpired on these pages are the actions I chose, coupled with God's blessing me and keeping me in his favor. Why would God keep me in his favor? It is because I acknowledge him as my God and Master, and I am his loyal servant.

I once got into a very interesting discussion with a patron who was having a cup of coffee at a local coffee shop. He was reading the Bible. After I got my cup of coffee, I walked over, smiled, and said, "A very good book." He agreed emphatically, and a conversation ensued. I found out he was the senior pastor at the local Lutheran church. Somehow, the conversation turned to sin. I said, "I firmly believe that all thoughts come from either Satan or God. We do not have original thoughts, unlike what most people would like to believe. Good thoughts come from God, and evil thoughts come from Satan. Since we have free will given us by God, all we can take credit for is what thoughts we choose to pursue. If we choose to pursue evil thoughts, we have been influenced by Satan, and we commit a sin. If we pursue good thoughts, we are influenced by God, and we do right." He aggressively disagreed with me and said that we as humans have inherent evil in us and hence can sometimes come up with sin all on our own.

The argument continued with no one acquiescing. Into the busy café walked a gentleman who the Lutheran pastor said hello to. He said, "Harry, I want you to meet Leo, and Leo, this is Pastor Harry from the local Methodist church." I smiled and shook Pastor Harry's hand. The Lutheran pastor then said to Pastor Harry, "Leo and

I have a disagreement. Would you please educate Leo about the fact that humans have sin within them?" The Lutheran pastor continued and explained our differences of opinion.

Harry, the Methodist pastor, thought for a while and said purposefully, "Leo is right." I immediately raised both my fisted hands in the air to acknowledge victory. Harry went on to say, "Adam and Eve were created pure and free of sin. It was Satan in the form of a snake that planted the evil thought in Eve's mind, and Eve, with her free will, chose to pursue that thought. From thence, as a punishment, we were relegated and born in sin. Now the Bible is full of stories and parables. The actual persona of Satan does not need to be a serpent. Neither does the actual violation of God's single tenet by Eve need to be a bite into an apple. Suffice it to say that Eve violated God's sole rule given to her by choosing the thought suggested by Satan, and she talked Adam into it as well. He also had a free will and chose to listen to his mate, Eve. And the rest, as they say, is history."

My father also was a God-fearing Christian man and a career Indian army officer. He served 37 years in the armed forces. In World War II, he fought as an Allied commander in Burma against the Japanese. He also served during the Indo-China aggression, as it was called, in 1962 and the two Pakistani wars in 1965 and 1971. He was a true World War II hero. In 1944, at the tail end of the war, he was injured because his Willys Jeep went over a land mine and flew 40 feet into the air. Minutes before the mishap, he switched places with the driver and started to drive because the driver was dosing. The soldier was killed instantly, and my father lay there for hours before an Allied officer discovered the wreck and took my dad to the military hospital. If my dad had not switched places with the driver, he would have died.

My dad came home on a stretcher. He spent the next 18 months on his back in a military hospital. The doctors said he would never walk again. One night as he was dozing, he saw a figure in a pure white robe leaning over him. He thought he had died and was being greeted by a heavenly being.

The man asked him, "Son, do you believe?"

My father replied, "Yes." The man then asked if he could pray for him and what he might want in the prayer.

My father said, "I would like to walk and meet my wife at the railroad station in two weeks when she comes to visit me." He had not walked or even sat up in 18 months.

The man prayed, "Father, if it is thy will, make this man walk in two weeks." Then he left. Two weeks later, my dad walked on crutches and met my mother at the railroad station. The man who prayed for my father was the famous Bishop Herbert Pakenham-Walsh who traveled far and wide praying over wounded soldiers.

My dad was the king of clichés when we were growing up. One cliché he often used was, "God helps those who help themselves." When I was young, I used to think my dad was a broken record because he repeated himself all the time with his clichés. Boy, was he 100 percent right about the clichés he drilled into me. They turned out to be spot on. Over time, it was uncanny; I saw all my father's clichés and advice come to fruition. They all started to materialize in my life. From the earliest time I can remember, I believed in God. However, now I don't believe, I simply know He exists. God is all about abundance, and He wants the best for us as long as we believe and put our trust in him all the way. I know this for a fact. If I do everything I need to do to get whatever I want to get, as long as I choose right and not wrong and don't willfully hurt another, God will bless me for my effort beyond my wildest dreams.

This God Principle is criteria-driven just like all principles are. All performers and achievers know that criteria are important when following principles in order to attain a goal. We all know that knowing a principle and adhering to it are two different things. Adhering to God Principles is much harder than just knowing them. Many Christians know a lot of God's principles. The challenge is following them, especially when the Architect of the principle is (1) not visible and (2) cannot be audibly heard most of the time. However, like most principles, if you neglect the tenet of the principle and don't believe in it, you're fresh out of luck. Let's face it. Adhering to the principle is downright difficult.

Here are the criteria for this God Principle:

1. You have to work your tail off—no ifs, ands, or buts.
2. You can and should set goals, but you cannot negotiate the time it will take for the God Principle to deliver your goals.

3. You must be 100 percent consistent in the effort department, even though the devil makes it seem like the effort you are committing to is in vain and you are wasting your time. You must never fall for that.
4. You must expect success.

These are not mere words I am writing to make you feel warm and fuzzy or to make you roll your eyes and say, "That is a bunch of malarkey." This is downright exciting stuff. The results of this God Principle have occurred repeatedly throughout my entire life. It is uncanny how 100 percent predictable this God Principle is.

Chapter 4

AN ABBREVIATED HISTORY OF MY CHILDHOOD THROUGH COLLEGE

Let's backtrack yet a bit more to give you some perspective on all of this. I graduated from high school just before my 16th birthday, not because I was brilliant. When I was growing up in India, a child didn't have to be six years old (as the law is these days) to enter elementary school. If you could spell *cat, ran, dog, rat,* and so on, you were admitted to school in the first grade. My mother was a teacher off and on when she wanted to be since she did not have to work. Most middle-class and upper-middle-class women in India didn't work in those days. She made sure her children (my two older sisters and I) knew how to read and write at a very early age. Thus, I got into first grade when

I was four years old and went right through school like a greased pig.

My mother was also a published author of short stories (she wrote in English). She was a linguist and spoke fluent French, English, and five Indian languages that all had different alphabets. She also just happened to be the lead soprano in all the churches and cathedrals we attended over the years. She was a true concert soprano with a marvelous timbre to her voice and a very sweet, subtle tremolo. She would sing clean, low notes like an alto and hit the highs like a trained soprano. She was not trained at all. She hit the high notes in a stellar way without screeching or sounding strained. Growing up with a lot of her tutelage, I learned how to sing harmony in the church choir. I also was a boy soprano before my voice changed, and I turned into a baritone soloist in the choir.

My first school, Doufton Corey High School, was a private British K–12 school in Madras (now known as Chennai) in the state that was also called Madras (now known as the state of Tamil Nadu). When Dad got transferred to a city called Jabalpur in central India, my sisters and I attended another parochial school called Christ Church High School, also a K–12 school. In fact, when I was growing up, most schools in India were K–12 schools. Then Dad got transferred to the famous city of Agra in the state of Utter Pradesh where the Taj Mahal is. There I attended St. George's High School. In early 1962, Dad got transferred to an ammunitions base, the largest in all of Asia, in a nondescript village called Pulgaon. We

AN ABBREVIATED HISTORY OF MY CHILDHOOD–COLLEGE

joined Dad in Pulgaon after the school year ended in Agra. It was a base with a very rudimentary school that taught in the vernacular. All the schools my sisters and I attended instructed in English.

During the summer of 1962, we went to my maternal grandparents' house in Punjab where my grandfather had bought a farm when he retired. On the farm, he built multiple brick and mortar buildings to house a full-blown school that taught people for free. In the early 1960s, illiteracy was a huge problem in India. My grandfather was passionate about educating the masses. The school was completely accredited by the government. The most unique thing about the school was that there were 25-year-olds in first grade studying side-by-side and learning with five-year-olds. It was an amazing program, and I don't believe it was ever replicated. Part of the funding came from my grandfather's classmates in the United States, but most of it was self-funded by the profits the farm generated. My grandfather could have been a wealthy farmer like the neighboring farmers. However, he chose to be upper middle class and used the extra money that would have made him wealthy to educate people for free.

Unbeknownst to me, my parents talked to my grandparents and decided I would stay there and attend the amazing Takana Farm High School for a year. My year on the farm was exciting as well as extremely difficult. It taught me at a very tender age many things that would help me throughout my life. I was 12 years old and in charge of the poultry farm with 3,000 birds. For my efforts working seven days a week, I was allowed to ride the horse when it was not being used for drawing the carriage. Though my grandfather owned a Land Rover with the spare tire on the hood and a windshield that swiveled forward, he loved riding in his very cool horse-drawn carriage.

Before attending classes that started at 9:00 a.m., I had to bike three miles from the house to the farm and sign off on all the eggs that were being delivered to five-star hotels in New Delhi. I also learned about how soil is tilled and sown with seed, how crops are irrigated and protected from pests, how crops are harvested, and finally how they are taken to market to turn into currency and a profit. It was a long process that required a tremendous amount of patience, faith, and delayed gratification. All of that would come in handy when I became an international businessman in my adult years.

After a year, I returned to Pulgaon. I was not excited about moving here, there, and everywhere, so I said something that sounded foolish at first but turned out to be very good. I told my parents, "Why don't you just send me to boarding school so I don't have to change schools all the time when Dad gets transferred?" My dad said that was a good idea, and I was admitted to St. John's, an all-boys Catholic boarding school in the city of Nagpur in the state of Maharashtra. As I said, I was not quite 16 when I graduated from high school at St. John's.

Nagpur was what we called a second-tier city. That meant it had a population of 3 million or less. I was

AN ABBREVIATED HISTORY OF MY CHILDHOOD–COLLEGE

admitted to St. Francis DeSales College in Nagpur. It was a sister institution to St. John's High School and in the same archdiocese. There was a huge push to make Indian males excel in science and math since it was the future. We were told that if we wanted to get a good job, getting a degree in science and math would ensure it. I have to hand it to my countrymen; they were right. Now, decades later, India dominates in engineering, medicine, science, and technology.

Life was very sexist all over the world in the 1960s, and India was hardly exempt. I triple majored in physics, chemistry, and mathematics. My class had 105 students, all with the same triple major. This fine class of 105 students had only four female students. Women mostly took home economics, history, social studies, literature, and philosophy. It was definitely sexist as far as subjects chosen by women were concerned. I also laugh at teachers in America's secondary schools who fight tooth and nail for classes with fewer than 25 students. They complain that they cannot properly attend to the personal needs of students in larger classes. With all their hullabaloo, these schools graduate pathetically inept students from high school day in and day out. With a ninth-grade education in the early 1960s, I could run circles around today's seniors from the public school system. I was in a class of more than 80 in a private Catholic boarding school—think about it. The Indians, Chinese, and Koreans are going to eat the Americans for lunch if Americans don't change things soon.

Chapter 5

DECISION TO VISIT THE USA

In 1919, my maternal grandfather was the first Indian (not the misnomer Indian whose correct nomenclature is Native American) to graduate from an American university. He traveled to the United States of America in 1911 via steamship and spent eight years in the USA. He was schoolmates and very close friends with a few students who went on to become very high-profile global personalities, including Paul Robeson, the famous baritone recording artist of "Ol' Man River" fame and Ellsworth Bunker, an American businessman and diplomat who was one of only two Americans to receive the Presidential Medal of Freedom twice and the only one to receive it with distinction. Interestingly, Bunker was the US Ambassador to India in the 1950s.

My grandfather was a very prolific individual, a God-fearing Christian and a very intellectually sound man of uncommon integrity who was a huge achiever. He graduated Phi Beta Kappa from Rutgers University when Rutgers was a good institution (tsk tsk tsk) with a PhD in English literature. He returned to India in 1919. In the 1940s, Mahatma Gandhi asked him to help develop the educational system in India in a program called Rural Uplift. When I was five years old, my grandfather told me that if I ever got a chance, I should visit America.

He further explained what a very special place America was. He went on to say, "The nation encourages independent thinking, and for that singular reason, the US is a fertile environment for human excellence."

I, being a precocious kid, asked my grandfather, "If America is such a special place, how come you returned to live in India?"

Without hesitating, he smiled and said, "To marry your grandmother, Son, so I could start a family and ultimately have you as my first grandson."

My five-year old brain was very satisfied with that answer. I guess that was when the seed was firmly planted in me to visit America. I heeded my grandfather's words and with much calculated evaluation decided to visit America.

The decision was firmly made early in my freshman year in college. What made a young kid with zero money have the guts or be foolish enough to make such a decision to visit America? Well, it was my unabashed belief in God that made me take that step. I truly believe that once an individual decides to pursue his or her dreams and is willing to use some elbow grease, roll

DECISION TO VISIT THE USA

up their sleeves, and work hard without negotiating the price, they will have to pay for that specific success and, in my case, believe in God. In turn, God will make their dreams come true. Oftentimes, God makes things happen in the most outlandish way. The way my dream was fulfilled was extremely outlandish. God completely made it possible for me to have enough and some left over to make that decision possible.

My father also instilled in me that I should always follow through on the decisions I make. I also relied heavily on my mind's God-given ability to evaluate things and make decisions. I seriously contemplated where I might want to live my life. Young Indian males from middle-class families did not have the luxury of contemplating where they would like to live. They were relegated to where they could get employment after they finished their education. The other thing about living in India as a young person was that you did not graduate and get a job and then quit the job to get a master's degree. There were no night programs, so you could not work and get a master's concurrently like many do today. After that, if you wanted a doctorate, you had to quit your job again to do that or work for a company that allowed you to do that while employed, and that, too, was not common. In India in the 1960s, if you decided to pursue further education, you did it straight through. To prove my point, just before leaving India for the USA, I was friends with a young 24-year-old. He had just gotten a PhD in agricultural engineering from the Pusa Institute of Agriculture in New Delhi. It was not uncommon for young adults to have a PhD in their mid to late 20s.

It was amazing how God worked through Ajay, a friend and choir mate of mine at All Saints Cathedral in Nagpur. You, the reader, will realize that my personal input in the whole process was rather simple. All I did was put in the incessant hard work I needed to do, and God made the rest fall into place. My work was similar to a farmer's. I equated all the work I did to a farmer tilling the soil, irrigating the land, sowing the seed, maintaining the crop by keeping pests and vermin away, and finally harvesting the crop and taking it to market. That was a huge effort the farmer made every season for each crop. I comprehended that process very well since I had spent a year on my grandfather's farm. Even though the farmer did a whole lot of work and believed he would prevail, there was no way he could make that crop grow. It was God who blessed the farmer with the growth of the crop he planted after all that preparation. God rewards hard work and commitment. When that harvest was sold, it converted to currency that allowed the farmer to have the quality of life he worked hard for. God did the same for me so I could achieve my dream and live the life I worked so hard for.

Chapter 6

WHY AMERICA?

Why America? There are two reasons. First, my grandfather told me that if I ever got a chance, I should visit America. Second, I was also a very political young man, like most idealistic students are. I weighed the different forms of government that existed and their pros and cons. And this was the paradox: Even though I had self-esteem, I was still full of insecurities and doubt about being able to make it. How was I going to become a successful person? What was I going to do?

I grew up in a very good family with strong values, a solid unshakable belief in God, and a no-nonsense approach to right and wrong. We had all we needed but not all we wanted. In short, we never had any excesses. Therefore, it was a given that none of us three siblings could ride on the financial coattails of our parents because they had no financial coattails to latch onto. We, like most of the populace in India, had to create or develop our own future or choke—another exercise in free will. We were blessed to have enough to be middle class in a third-world country. It's worth noting that middle class in India back then was living at a lower standard than welfare in the United States where people had an apartment, refrigeration, hot and cold water, heat, air conditioning, sometimes black and white and subsequently color TV, and a car.

It blows my mind when liberals all around the world, especially in the USA, pretend to care. Their pseudo fight for the rights of the minority is based on people not having anything willed to them, and thus society owes them something. That is such utter nonsense. These same people will throw a fit if their upper-class offspring brought a person from the ghetto home for Thanksgiving only to declare they have plans to marry.

There are billions of people on earth and tens of millions in the United States that have nothing willed to them, and that is absolutely a reality. Ironically and hypocritically, a serious fact remains. Liberals have controlled too many blighted cities in the United States for decades, and a lot of the minorities have not changed one iota throughout those decades of liberal rule. Even though liberals always promise them the moon in order to get their votes, they deliver nothing—*ever*. Liberal politicians are like Christians who attend church on Easter and Christmas. They only care for the people during elections. The rest of the time, these so-called caring individuals don't want to be associated with the minorities who are struggling. The reason the blighted cities controlled by liberals are still blighted after decades of rule is because liberal politicians are bold-faced liars. They will say anything to get elected.

Over the years, they have dumbed down the masses very cunningly through the educational system, from secondary school to the universities. They are just like the oppressive regimes of the world that brainwash people into thinking a dictatorship is a great form of government, that communism is for the good of all, or that a monarchy is just fine. The liberals do it in a very sophisticated, subtle way. They pretend to throw money at them and promise free this or that. They always leave their constituencies with unfulfilled promises. They make sure they sound warm and fuzzy, but in actuality, they are totally hollow. The minorities are just waking up to this fact after decades and are realizing that they have been played for the past three to four generations. Since this is in the early stages, minority voices are not so rampant. So liberals are on a campaign to shun, belittle, abuse, and shame the minorities into silence.

My two older sisters and I were given a lot of love, a sense of, "I can do anything I put my mind to," and a good education. That is all you really need. This whole thing about parents not wanting their children to go through what they went through is producing a bunch of namby-pamby adults who will be crushed by competition from India, China, South Korea, and Japan.

The attitude of, "I can do anything I set my mind to,"

was untested since we were still living at home and not earning a living. I started to think very deeply about where I should live. This was an uncommon thought process for a 16-year-old freshman attending college. Most 16-year olds in India were focusing on their studies and having a good time while they could. After graduating, they got a job, and the next time they came up for air was when they retired. I found that to be society's brainwashing. I was not going to partake in that paradigm. I saw a job as being on a human conveyor belt to benefit industry, organizations, and government. I agree that the conveyor belt is crucial for modern societies. However, I prefer how things were during the nineteenth century. The majority of people owned a business of some sort. Now, we all have been sold the myth of the stellar plan of 40–45 years on that conveyor belt. And after that, whoopie! We can all retire on a third of an income that didn't cut the mustard when it was 100 percent. Through the years, we donate to Social Security, and the government devours it just like the operator of a Ponzi scheme, leaving Social Security to currently exist on borrowed money. On top of that, the government gives the donor (the general public) less of a return on their 40–45 years of being a donor to Social Security than what they would have gotten as a return if they had privately invested that money.

I realized I was different from the masses in India. The difference was the values with which I was brought up and the way I thought. None of my thoughts would have had any traction if it was not for the strict upbringing I lived through. There was no talking back. Rules set by my parents were nonnegotiable as long as we lived at home. The home we lived in belonged to our parents; it did not belong to us. That was made very clear in actual words, not just implied. Our parents decided what they wanted to do, and we, as part of the family, did it. We children did not have a vote. On occasion, we were considered. But being considered did not mean we could change the direction our parents decided. At best, we could influence it, and that was extremely rare. Being considered was a rare exception.

Dr. Spock would have been chased out of my parents' house. My parents loved us and treated us with dignity. However, excuses, nonsense, and breaking the rules were not tolerated. Our parents were acutely cognizant of raising us right. They raised us to stand on our own in a tough and competitive world. There was a lot of love, though, and due to that love, I never felt controlled or manipulated by my parents. Of course, there were times that I (an immature male) thought they were unreasonable when I wanted to do or have something they would not allow me to do or have. However, that is something all children encounter while growing up.

Fast-forward to my 16-year-old brain. I started to analyze things because I was going to make a very serious decision about where I was going to live. It was such an off-the-wall consideration. Wealthy people in free societies thought about where they would live because the money they had made them flexible. Middle-class people in free societies lived where they could, and a percentage of them visited foreign lands. The majority of them only moved because of a job, and that could very well be a place they didn't want to live. However, money made the decision for them.

I want to say this as an aside. If only people, everyday people, would give their brain the respect it deserves and use it to its fullest capacity by just thinking, its amazing power and ability would blow their minds every single time. It sure blew mine. It is truly amazing what your mind can come up with if it is used properly and consistently. A mind is one of the most powerful instruments a human possesses. And, like all powerful instruments, we need to learn to use it and use it correctly in every instance and circumstance.

A powerful instrument can hurt an individual when it is used improperly. It is also a waste of an amazing asset when it is not used at all. There is a saying that goes like this: Common sense is not common at all. I have never heard the reason why that is so. I thought about it and have come up with a very plausible reason. People either graduate from college, go to trade school, or join the workforce after high school. They are usually eager when they first start their lives and are ready to learn. The mind is alert and ready to absorb and implement. Of course, I am speaking generally here. A few years down the road, they settle in because they have been doing the same thing repeatedly and can do it in their sleep. Now, the majority relaxes (as we as humans love to relax) and puts themselves on autopilot. They stop reading books, and if they do read, they read trash. They watch the news and regurgitate it like they are experts. They watch low IQ TV. This is a prescription for an individual to become totally void of common sense.

People do not realize a simple, amazing fact about the mind. Many individuals who are seemingly intellectually sound live mindless lives without really planning or setting goals. Let me give you some perspective. I used my young, so-called inexperienced mind to make a huge decision. It still amazes me how good God is. He helped me make solid, untested decisions when I put my trust in him. I want to state something categorically. The decision I made was not a fluke. The reason it was not a fluke is because I analyzed it deeply and seriously, and God helped me come to a solid conclusion. After reaching a conclusion, I then made a quality decision and set a goal. I then did the most critical thing to realize the goal. I acted on it. It was way too thought-out to be a fluke. It is what I would call a concerted decision. Concerted decisions cannot be fluke decisions. I will give you a brief overview of how my then 16-year-old brain, assisted by God, weighed all the various options and came to that momentous conclusion of where I was ultimately going to live.

My political mind was not going to consider weather, geography, proximity to my family, or a host of emotional things that hold most people back. It is amazing how compromised your life is when you stay close to where you were born due to emotional decisions. Stay close to where you were born if it is the right decision. However, do not stay just to be close to family. You can be anywhere in the world in a day. I was going to decide and go wherever I had to, do whatever I had to, so I could live the life I wanted. Given that government plays an important, integral role in everyone's quality of life or lack thereof, choosing the right type of government where I was going to live was the most pivotal factor in my decision. So job one was to evaluate the various types of governments that existed in the world. I came up with five basic forms of government.

1. Monarchy
2. Dictatorship
3. Democracy
4. Communism
5. Socialism (I call it communism in sheep's clothing—a blatant euphemism, if you will)

I grew up in a very old civilization that was a very young democratic society. India had recently gotten its freedom. It had been a colony under a massively successful global monarchy—England. It was a given that I was not a big fan of a monarchy. I do not subscribe to a society that allows one individual to control masses of humanity just because he or she was fermented in the right testicles. I am sorry for the graphic visual here, but isn't what I just said a true, raw fact? In short, the criteria for a monarchy did not sit well in my brain. Sometimes, stark graphic statements like the one I just made tend to jar people and bring things to light in a very clear way. Hence, I categorically ruled out a monarchy.

A dictatorship is basically a monarchy gone wrong. In this form of governance, we have one individual who controls the masses, not just with the threat of violence as a remedy for anyone who fails to follow stringent and often oppressive laws and regulations but one that is oftentimes weighted in favor of the ruling class. It is one who actually kills, rapes, maims, and brutalizes citizens who do not toe the line in totality. Hence, I categorically ruled out a dictatorship.

Socialism is a play on words and thus a mind game. I simply abhor mind games. Socialism is communism in sheep's clothing, pretending to care about the masses but extremely brutal with a smiling demeanor and a soft-spoken voice with a warm, fuzzy content that will never—I repeat never—be realized. This form of governance took away the very thing my grandfather spoke about that made the US such a great society. Socialism under the guise of caring for all took away independent thinking and thus oppressed people from the core. Hence, I categorically ruled out socialism.

Democracy was something I comprehended well. However, it was extremely disappointing that corruption abounded in India and the judiciary was not strong. The High Court (India's Supreme Court) was like a puppet of the politicians. On a rare occasion, it would do something and excite the general public, and then it would return to business as usual. The politicians ran amuck, and corruption was rampant from the cop on the beat to the nation's prime minister. One interim prime minister was in office for 10 months, and from already being worth millions of dollars from public stealing, he increased his net worth during those months to the tune of $100 million US dollars. I truly had nothing to compare our Indian democracy to since I had lived in India all my life. Reading only takes you so far. So democracy was not out; it was just on hold to evaluate the last serious form of government left—communism.

Communism looked awesome on paper if you are into warm and fuzzy rhetoric that turns offensive on a dime after power is assumed. Everyone has a place to live, everyone has a job, everyone has health care, everyone has an income. Communism was in short a political system for the common good of all—not the individual. I say this: We screwed up the common good of all the minute Eve bit into that proverbial apple. To me, communism was like the sandbox principle of sharing. However, as usual, the ones who ran the show, even though they spoke of common good, lived high on the hog for their good. They had all the trappings of royalty but constantly reminded the populace that it was for the office and not the person in the office. However, the person in the office never left. On the other hand, the masses shared the not-enough funds generated by the government's printed money that kept being worth less every year.

We should remember unequivocally that governments do not—I repeat *do not*—generate revenue; they merely print revenue. Only private, incentive-driven, market-controlled enterprises generate revenue—*period*. China would still be a crummy economy if it were not for the capitalistic reforms it has made. Only capitalism is a true and tested form of government that actually enhances the standard of living and quality of life of the hard working. The downside is that sluff-offs get beat in a capitalistic society and cause the most amount of noise. We all have friends, relatives, and acquaintances who talk way too much and do nothing or very little. We must understand that in a capitalistic society, behavior of the type that talks too much and does the minimum or nothing at all will ensure a lower middle-class life. On the other hand, any life in a capitalistic society ensures a better quality of life than that of socialism, communism, a dictatorship, or a monarchy. We should also understand that England is not at all a monarchy. It is just not able to relieve itself of its monarchs due to emotional issues, and that is its prerogative.

Anywhere on earth, a thinking person always takes very good care of what is important to their well-being. Most politicians are so utterly stupid that they don't understand this basic principle of protecting one's well-being. Their well-being is solely created by enterprises that directly create the GDP (gross domestic product), the net worth, if you will, of a nation's economy. The GDP, in turn, generates taxes that keep politicians in power. So you would think that politicians would protect enterprises all day long because they are the root that grows the revenue tree that generates the very cash that sustains them. Wrong! They tear down enterprises in a losing rhetoric to get the vote. It is so warm and fuzzy to tell the masses, "You need free health care, you need free college tuition, you need subsidized housing (which is partially free), and on and on and on. Sounds good until you realize that $52 trillion for 10 years will buy health care for all and nothing else. That is $5.2 trillion per year, just for health care, when the entire US federal budget is currently $4.1 trillion. What is hilarious is that politicians actually think they can do better with money than private enterprise can.

You see, this again is a God Principle. What you release will in turn create more of it. That means releasing or giving will actually increase the very thing you release or give. You see, it has to do with the principle of sowing and reaping. We all know that a seed has to die in order to produce a mother lode of seeds. Similarly, enterprises know that sowing money into their businesses (which seems like killing money for a non-enterprise individual) actually produces more money. Sowing money into their businesses for expansion, new jobs, and the upgrading of equipment creates a stronger economy, which in turn creates more revenue for consumer goods, housing, savings, and investments, and the cycle feeds itself. Politicians have no clue about this principle whatsoever. If given free rein, the politicians' principles of government (which know not how to multiply revenue) eventually would dry up the flow of money. That pathetic philosophy created the USSR, the old China, and Cuba where the masses lived below poverty levels. It created North Korea, which routinely ran out of food every winter, and it created the Venezuelas of the world.

Hence, due to a lack of real revenue generated by the non-existence of incentive-driven private enterprise, people in communist or socialist countries share a diminishing pot of revenue. One could ask, why not print as much money as needed if that is the case. Too much revenue (currency) being printed would literally tank the economy even faster. When the USSR annexed Eastern Europe, it managed to run a crummy, fake, printed money economy for 69 years from 1922 to 1991. The ruble was not as good as toilet paper outside the USSR. You might ask, "Why do you say that?" Well, toilet paper works everywhere on earth. The ruble didn't. China would have folded a while back if it had not become a pseudo-capitalistic society. Now, Communist China is aggressively showing its political ugliness by the way it is coming down hard on Hong Kong, its best gateway city to the international markets. Talk about a host of leaders in China being utterly *stupid*! See how stupid politicians are when given free rein?

The sad thing is that humans have a tremendous amount of tolerance, and tolerance is sometimes not a good thing. Mike Murdock, who has written scores of books and is a person I have interacted with on a very deep level, says (and I paraphrase): That which you tolerate, you must live with. You see, the longer you tolerate something unsavory, the nastier it gets. Things that could have been resolved at a very early, insignificant level all of a sudden become a huge problem. As a result, we overreact and erupt due to pent-up emotions that have developed due to tolerance.

When we tolerate something insignificant for too long, it is not a good thing. Remember the *Tale of Two Cities* that depicted the French Revolution? Remember the coup that exiled the Shah of Iran and installed the Khomeini? A coup d'état or a revolution usually is a direct result of tolerating an oppressive government for far too long. Everything could be resolved in a much better manner if only things were nipped in the bud. The reason things got so out of hand and violent, which ultimately ushered in the French Revolution, was because the masses were abused far too long and tolerated it way too long. They finally could not take it anymore, and the result was a bloody revolution.

So finally my decision came down to the two heavies: communism and democracy. Like all good analysts, I put the two forms of government side-by-side on a piece of paper. I drew a line all the way down the middle, dividing them from each other. I then made a head-on comparison.

Democracy	Communism
Guarantees religious freedom	Bans religious freedom
Guarantees political freedom	Bans political freedom
Does not guarantee personal finance	Guarantees minimal personal finance

Pondering the above tenets was very revealing. Communism guarantees a tepid personal economy, and you don't have to worry about being homeless, jobless, or worthless. However, it suspends two important freedoms: religious freedom and political freedom.

Democracy guarantees religious freedom and political freedom but does not guarantee any personal finance. For finances, you're on your own in a democracy. These two predominant forms of government turned out to be diametrically opposed to each other at the core. So a clear choice was not going to be hard to make.

The statement I am about to make is going to rub some people the wrong way. However, reality is often harsh and hard to stomach. The truth hurts sometimes. Analyzing a bit deeper, I personally concluded this: The majority of an entire society must have low self-esteem if they want a government to guarantee them an income and an existence. We must always understand that the entity that guarantees a person an income will invariably control the person to whom it guarantees an income. It does not matter if it is an individual, an organization, a corporation, or a government that guarantees the individual an income. That entity will control them either overtly or covertly. The point is to identify that you are, in fact, being controlled and then ponder what you might decide to do about it. You either accept the control on the terms of the controller or decide to not accept the control and move on. I cannot stand people accepting the control and then constantly complaining, moaning, and groaning about it.

If moving on is the decision you make, it hardly has to be easy or smooth. In fact, it is often wrought with hurdles, challenges, and downright pressure. The fact that it is some or all of the above should never dissuade a person from moving on if that is what they feel they want to do. Also realize that some people like being controlled and do not like being self-reliant. While they don't like being controlled, they lack the tenacity and guts to move on.

When a government is given free rein, as in a communist system, that is the epitome of control. Citizens hand control over to the government, and by doing so, they categorically relinquish almost all their fundamental rights. It gives the government the supreme power to suspend any or all the freedoms citizens are born with. All this is done under the guise of giving them a job, a compromised shelter, compromised health care, and some semblance of security with a less than rudimentary infrastructure. The freedoms I mention help control the masses, and most governments think in terms of masses, not individuals. Hence, communist governments have the power to suspend religious freedom, political freedom, freedom of speech, freedom to organize, freedom of the press, freedom to protest, freedom of the written word, and more.

Communist countries make it their business to control every freedom that humans were endowed with from God, just by guaranteeing them a pitiful living. The citizens are to blame for agreeing to accept below average as their living standard. That is one reason that communist and socialist governments do not like people who believe in the existence of God. That would mean people would believe they were endowed with inalienable rights and free will. That would encourage the overthrow of the oppressive communist government. So communism vehemently suspends the freedom to worship and have a belief in God. You will find that socialism in Europe is doing that as well in a covert way. They do it with the theory of evolution. I ask a simple question: Who is it that decides which species will evolve and which species will remain the same for tens of millions of years?

The irony is that all laws, whether in a communist country, a monarchy, a democracy, or even a dictatorship, are deeply rooted in the Ten Commandments. Bring me any law on earth, and I will tie it to the Ten Commandments. Yet in America, the left has a lot of activism against displaying the Ten Commandments in public places under the guise of separation of church and state.

Our founding fathers kept church and state separate not because they didn't want the government to acknowledge the church. In fact there are many instances where the church was the reason government was formed the way it was. For example, in order to incorporate a town in New England (that was the beginning of the USA as we know it), there had to be an established church or there would be no town. That was the criterion—*period*. The reason the founding fathers separated church and state was so a predominant religion could not force its beliefs and values on people by passing laws. They wanted to make sure ad infinitum that there would be true freedom of religion and worship. The left is so far off from the truth that it is madness. Many argue that the Ten Commandments must not be displayed in public places. Does anyone realize that the Ten Commandments are the cornerstones of our republic and the US Constitution is founded on the belief that God is, in fact, the supreme power? The words "unalienable rights" are a direct reference to God.

Atheists are amazingly threatened by the Ten Commandments. If I were an atheist, I would not care about people displaying them. As an atheist, it would not matter to me that there are people who believe. It would only matter to me that I don't believe. In fact, as an atheist, I would look at people who believe in God as interesting and not threatening at all. If I didn't believe in God, why on earth would I be threatened by someone who believes? In fact, if I were an atheist, I would know there is no God and that the competition was spending way too much time acknowledging, praying, and revering what is not. That would be good for me as an atheist. I would be spending so much more time doing things that get me ahead of those fantasy pushers who spend such inordinate amounts of time on a fictitious non-being *Being*.

It is pretty much the same when I see a person who drives a car with a hundred stickers on it. I am not offended by that at all. I am intrigued at best. My personal observation is that some people cannot verbalize their point of view for one reason or another and have a compulsion to let the world know how they feel. So they pepper their automobile with stickers that deliver their views. Then there is the fact that oftentimes, it is intellectually cool to have a socially warm and fuzzy message sticker on your car. The sad thing is that for these people, they have the sticker but are not really sold or passionate about what the sticker is all about.

For example, anything about going green is a very cool sticker to have on your vehicle. Everyone is impressed. However, if you go to the house of the person with the sticker on their car, you will find them using detergents that are toxic to the waterways and ecologically far from good. You will find with many of them that their heat is on high in the winter, and their air conditioner is on high in the summer. They also have a huge SUV in their driveway as their second car, and they waste food every week either in their disposal or by throwing it away in their garbage. When you talk to them, you would never know they are the same people with that oh so warm and fuzzy sticker on their car. Numerous people don't live the message their sticker proclaims.

I once saw a woman with the multicultural, multireligious sticker with the different symbols spelling COEXIST. I am sure you have seen them; they have been around since hippies wandered the face of the earth. She honked and flipped this guy the bird because he had the audacity to slide into ample space in front of her in traffic. That is really coexisting, right?

Let's get back to communism. People who believe in God put God first, their family second, and their country third. This is unacceptable by an insecure communist government that wants to control people and stay in power indefinitely. Hence, banning religious freedom tops the list, and political freedom is either equal to or a very close second.

I have always had a very healthy self-esteem (despite the fact that I, like many, was put down a lot throughout my young life by a few family members, friends, superiors, and strangers alike. I never let it phase me, though. My father said, "Just because someone calls you something does not mean you are that something." He also said, "Just because someone treats you poorly does not connote that you are someone who should be treated poorly. They do not have the power to speak you into or out of who the core you is. Be sure you strive to be the best you that you can be. Be careful who you acknowledge and who you ignore. Most of the noise out there makes no sense. It is up to you to decipher the noise that is irrelevant and the noise that is not."

I have had people ask how I know what makes sense and what does not. To that I say, "Think." God has given us an amazing mind, and if we lean on him for wisdom, we will unequivocally have it. The wisdom God provides us will enable us to weigh key issues and come to wise conclusions. Our job is to get all sides of an issue, do due diligence, and evaluate things logically. When we do make mistakes, consider them merely steps on the ladder of success. Never stop trying because of the fear of making mistakes. Behavior of this sort guarantees mediocrity at best.

I was not going to let anyone dictate my future to me, and neither should you. No one has control over my joy, my happiness, or my future but me. I only paid attention to people who had what I wanted. It is pretty simple.

If you want to major in physics, you attend a lecture given by a physics professor. Oh, Leo! Can't I attend a lecture by a chemistry professor instead? C'mon, they are both academics of high value. What difference does it make? My answer, which is obvious, in one word is "Monumental."

If you want to learn golf, learn it from a golf pro and not a tennis pro. Sure, they are both good athletic individuals. They both have an instrument that hits a ball with great skill. However, their swings vary greatly, and therein lies the huge difference.

Many people seek professional or relationship advice from a friend or family member who has no clue what they are talking about. They feel that because this friend or family member has a respected position in a company, has achieved a good level of success in a certain field, or has their respect as an individual, they will surely know things outside their sphere of expertise. Not true.

I am going to iterate a true story. In the mid-1990s, I was working with a couple to help them develop a business. He was a pilot. He flew left seat (he was the captain) for a major airline, and she was a special education teacher. Like a lot of couples, they were going through some tough times in their marriage that were routinely solvable. However, the woman asked her female friend for advice. This friend just happened to have been divorced three times and was at that time in a crappy, dead-end relationship that was going nowhere (which she stated publicly on numerous occasions). The three-time loser strongly and categorically told the woman seeking marital advice that if it were her, she would leave him. After a few months, instead of working out the problems in her 22-year marriage, she sued for divorce on the advice of her foolish friend. She got divorced, and decades later she is still single. I know she is not very happy. Her husband, on the other hand and to her utter chagrin, married a considerably younger flight attendant, moved on, and is fine.

The takeaway is that if you want advice, get the proper information from the proper source, weigh the consequences of the pros and cons, and make up your own mind. Your mind was given to you by God, and he did not give you a deficient mind. When used, your mind is the most capable thing you have. However, the mind is like everything else. If left unused, it becomes worthless and stubborn in its paradigm. There is a saying that a mind functions like a parachute—it works only when open.

In my life, only God had the right to direct my future. However, God also gave me the right of free will. This right allowed me to choose to either follow God's direction or Satan's. There is no other option. Everyone—believers, agnostics, and atheists—have but two choices: a good decision, which is always God-driven, or a bad decision, which is always Satan-driven. Whether you believe or not, that is the be-all and end-all of everything, always. Whether you accept that or not does not really matter. It is what it is—a rather simple reality actually.

I decided at a very young age that I was not willing to forego all my freedoms to have someone else allow me this oh so minimal standard of living under the guise of a nation built for all. So communism, too, was unequivocally out.

I was left with democracy. Hmm! I decided I liked the guarantee of religious and political freedoms way too much and was nervously confident that I—yes, the little untested me—could develop my own personal finances (income). I was right. I have generated my own income for the past 48 years and have never asked a soul for money or financial assistance since I graduated from college.

Now, knowing what I know, I never will rely on any government for money. In fact, it is completely the other way around. All governments, bar none, rely on their populace for money. Remember, they work for you, and we must never get complacent about reminding the government and the politicians that they work specifically for us and should take their jobs seriously. To the best of their abilities, they should run a tight and good government that does not take away personal freedoms, no matter what.

Talk softly, talk loudly, or even scream if you have to. But never let the government get away with doing a lousy job. If a baseball player has an awkward style but scores runs or throws strikes, do you care about style?

Similarly, vote for people who can deliver results. Don't get caught up in the style and lose all substance. With the advent of the Internet, satellite TV, and social media, the simpletons are voting style, and the politicians are capitalizing on it. I say that is absolutely the wrong thing to do. Vote substance and not style, gender, or color.

I just happened to live in the largest democracy in the world—India. So why not stay there? It was safe, and I could at the very least be middle class in an environment that was extremely familiar to me. The question was, could I live with the disgusting, rampant corruption that existed in India while I was growing up there? Most people accepted the corruption by looking the other way. They said things like, "Lighten up, Leo, or you're going to have a heart attack." If I brought up the condition of the country, the majority always said, "C'mon, you cannot do anything about it. You just gotta work around it."

I decided I could not and would not work around it if I could help it. To stay there would be the easy way out as far as decisions go. However, it would compromise my values, and I would have to put up with the political nonsense going on in India in the 1960s. Most people unfortunately take the easy way out, and that guarantees them mediocrity at best. Hell, no, I was not going to take the easy way out. I was not going to be mediocre; I was going to excel.

I learned very early that easy does not pay that well, and hard pays very well. David in the Old Testament was paid very well for taking on the insurmountable task of killing Goliath, a seemingly impossible and daunting task. It was not easy. In fact, it was so daunting that no one else even considered it, for crying out loud. Saul had a strong army with battle-hardy warriors, and none of them—I repeat, none of them—wanted to even consider taking on Goliath. Even in those days, there was a fake press, and it got to them. Who was the fake press in King Saul's time? They were the Philistines, Goliath's clan. They taunted the Hebrews night and day leading up to the deadline of the famed contest. With their propaganda, they were trying to intimidate the Hebrews, and they almost succeeded.

Close, but no cigar! David was not going to take the easy way out. For not taking the easy way out and achieving the monumental task of killing Goliath, David got King Saul's daughter in marriage and ultimately became king of the united kingdom of Israel and Judah. None of it would have happened if young, ruddy, shepherd boy David, the youngest son of Jesse, had used his free will to make the wrong decision and take the easy way out. I could get off track and go on and on with authentic prose from both the Old and New Testaments about how *hard* always paid extremely well, and easy never did. However, since this is not a religious story, I will stay on point and refer to God only when I feel it's necessary since he just happens to hold the highest esteem and is the most integral part of my life.

Next, I went about the task of evaluating democracies. The most successful democracy in the world was the USA. Aha! My grandfather's words rang out in my ears. "If you ever get a chance, visit America, Son." Also, since

HARD WORK AND THE AMERICAN DREAM

I was a musician, I said to myself that the Beatles were not the Beatles until they went to America. In fact, all the greats needed to have a footprint in America if they wanted to be serious global players, or they were just going to be regional bit players in the world. So I made my decision. I was going to visit America to evaluate the country for myself. Remember, I made this decision when I had no income and zero financial assets. The principle is to *dream* first and then ask for God's help and support. After that, you work your tail off with a plan of action that always—I repeat, always—moves you toward your dream.

Chapter 7

ACQUIRING THE FINANCES TO ACHIEVE MY DREAM

One Sunday in 1967 when I was still in my freshman year of college, my friend Ajay, the bishop's second son (Anglican clergy do marry) and I were walking out of church. He turned to me and said, "Hey, Leo! Let's go to Modern Book Store." We were both in the choir. He was a tenor, and I was a baritone. He was a freshman doing pre-med, so I naturally assumed that he wanted to buy some textbooks.

I said, "Ajay, why don't you just go to the library and save the money?"

"Stupid," he said, "haven't you heard of the rock and roll music contest that Simla Cigarettes is having?"

Simla was a huge cigarette and tobacco products manufacturer in those days. I said no, and Ajay said, "Let's go fill out an application form to enter the competition."

I laughed out loud and said, "Ajay, you are the stupid one here. Why on earth would we want to fill out an application form to compete?"

"So we can compete, Stupid," he said, laughing incredulously.

"This is off-the-wall, ridiculous behavior," I said. "We don't have a band, we have substandard instruments, we have no real gear, we really have nothing, and you want to fill out a form to compete?"

He was not going to give up. He said in a very matter-of-fact way, "We have five months to figure all that out."

Before I knew it, we were walking into Modern Book Store. Ajay walked up with great gusto to the cashier and authoritatively asked where the applications forms were for the Simla Cigarettes Rock & Roll Contest. The cashier bent down and from under the counter pulled out a form and handed it to Ajay who was fired up. I was amazed at this utter nonsense.

Ajay said with an excited, high-pitched voice and a wide grin, completely animated, "What is the band's name going to be?"

"What?" I said. I was totally beside myself at this point. This was complete tomfoolery, and I was not laughing.

"C'mon, c'mon, c'mon," he said. You're really good at coming up with catchy stuff. You can come up with a name."

I decided to play along with this ridiculous behavior and said, "Okay. The Spitfires."

"That sounds awesome!" he said. "How did you just like that come up with that name, the Spitfires?"

"You know I'm a military brat, right? Well, that was a legendary British fighter aircraft used during World War II."

Ajay said, "Okay, I like that a lot. It is very good."

So just like that, we named this fictitious, make-believe band that had no real members the Spitfires. The band was born and on its way. It had two ragtag members, one that sang and played keyboard (Ajay) and one that sang and played rhythm guitar (me).

Over the next two weeks, we recruited Anil, a drummer and college mate of mine who was one year older than I was; Clive, a bass guitarist and graduate student studying law at Nagpur University; Zac, a lead guitarist from Singapore and also a pre-med student at my college; and Mr. D'Souza, a saxophonist who was a 62-year-old veteran musician of Portuguese descent who played at all the New Year's Eve dances held by the Catholic community. C'mon now, I had to have a bluesy sax player to do some cool stuff, right?

It was my first foray into developing a team and being a leader. I took charge of this new venture at the tender age of 16. I never knew how this amazing experience (along with the deeply ingrained values my dad and mom had instilled in me) would transform me into a wheeling, dealing musician. All of these experiences were going to be uber instrumental in molding me into who I was going to become down the road. God was working his potter's wheel and molding a young boy with dreams.

Cutting right to the chase, five months down the road, we won the citywide open competition. We made the front page of the *Nagpur Times* and the *Hitvada*, the two main local newspapers. It was both exciting and surprising that we won. Like everyone out there just starting out, we were hardly self-assured of anything but participating and being acknowledged locally. As most people are initially, we were, in fact, full of doubt, but the saving grace was that we were extremely passionate about what we were doing.

After the win and the publicity we got, I realized something that had never happened to me before. People who had attended the concert, strangers to me, stopped me in public places to congratulate me and spoke to me as if we had been friends for a long time. Girls! My goodness, girls came out of the woodwork because overnight we had become local celebrities. Since I was the lead singer and the talkative front man of the band, I got an extra dollop of popularity. Overnight, the band was the topic of conversation. Once, I overheard people in a coffee shop say something like this: "Have you heard? These local college students came from nowhere and did very well in that Rock & Roll Contest the Simla Cigarette Company held recently." "You know, they call themselves the Spitfires." "I am not sure what that name signifies, but the local fellas did very well."

This was a lot of fun. It's worth noting that there was no TV in India in 1967. If someone did not attend the competition, know one of the band members personally, or see the newspaper the next morning, they wouldn't recognize us in public. People were talking about the band, and every so often, we overheard conversations about us. They didn't know we were band members in their midst. To add to this newfound excitement, we were advised by the organizers of the competition what the next step was. We were officially given the dates to compete in the regional contest.

More excitement and more trepidation followed. To our surprise, we competed and won the regional competition as well. With that came more exposure and more fame. I was singled out and named best lead singer in the Western music (not to be mistaken for Country Western music) category. Wow! While I got maybe 25 percent of my mother's voice, I was the only member of the family to actually make money using it. It was heady stuff. It also got a bit nerve-racking because of what was to come next.

We were then slated to compete in the statewide competition, which was monumental. The state we were in was Maharashtra. The capital of Maharashtra was Bombay (now known as Mumbai). All the band members, including me, believed this competition was a foregone conclusion and was going to be very lopsided. Here we were, a local ragtag band of nobodies from Nagpur up against the movie industry (later to be known as Bollywood). You know how Bollywood got its name, right? B was for Bombay, and it was the Hollywood of the East. We were five wet-behind-the-ears teenage college kids and a 62-year-old sax player going up against the big guns in Bombay's entertainment machine. We felt we would inevitably be trounced and humiliated. Yet we needed to compete.

HARD WORK AND THE AMERICAN DREAM

I told the band that even if we lose, we will get some national exposure, and who knows what that could lead to. Man alive, what happened next was the God Principle playing out in earnest. We won in Bombay and were number one in the state of Maharashtra. Oh my goodness! The underdogs actually beat out a massive field of big dogs to become the best of the best in the state. It was like the Red Sox beating the Yankees in seven games for the pennant on their way to the World Series in 2004 against the St. Louis Cardinals, which they swept in four games. The warm-up pennant win was much bigger and way harder both mentally and physically than the ultimate World Series win. It was a much tougher hurdle to scale than the World Series, if you will. Hence, the pennant turned out to be a much juicier win than the World Series.

I related to the Red Sox win because it was the same for us in 1968. The state competition turned out to be a much juicier win than the national competition. The media was abuzz with the upset win in Bombay by a bunch of upstarts. Pictures of us flashed across the nation, and we were known. I was amazed at the way things progressed. Next, the Spitfires went on to win the all-India competition. All of a sudden, we were the number-one live rock and roll and rhythm and blues act in India.

This whole process, from the time we filled out that momentous application form at the Modern Book Store until the time we won the all-India contest, took about 15 months. During the middle of this craziness, I had

ACQUIRING THE FINANCES TO ACHIEVE MY DREAM

to give my board exams and pass my freshman year in college. You might ask, "What board exams?" Well, in India in those days, two exams (freshman year and senior year) in a bachelor's degree program were board exams. The papers were set in a different state than the one the student resided in and took the exam in. It was corrected in yet a different state so there was no hanky-panky in the exam and grading process.

The entire system was run on roll numbers issued by the state. You had no names on your papers in order to ensure anonymity and zero partiality. Roll numbers would prevent all preferential treatment, and thus the grades would be awarded on pure merit. The results were published in the statewide newspaper. If you saw your roll number in print, it meant you failed. That was where I learned that excuses don't count and warranted for nothing in life. You were responsible for your own successes or failures—*period*. Long before Nike's Just Do It tagline, I comprehended that process very clearly. My mantra to myself was, "Shut up, Leo. Just do what you need to do, and God will do the rest." With that attitude, I never saw my roll number in print. Life was and still is very exciting but also extremely tough at the same time. However, my mantra trumped all of it. I, with my mantra and God's blessings, overcame and prevailed.

Meanwhile, back to the God Principle, The Spitfires were hot. We were featured in a multiple-page article in the *Junior Statesman*. It was the Rolling Stone magazine of India during the 1960s and 1970s. Everyone who was anyone in the music business and all who appreciated

Western music knew the Spitfires. Over the next year, I became adept at negotiating contracts and making deals. We did not have any legal representation or fancy accountants. I ran all the legal stuff by Clive, my bass guitar player, who was in law school. The business stuff, scheduling, and negotiating contracts, I handled.

Accounting was simple. No matter what happened, we split the money six ways after we paid expenses. This entire amazing experience would mold me professionally and come in handy later on when I decided to become a businessman. We started playing in all the heavy venues—nightclubs and private clubs that were gambling clubs (there were no casinos in India). We also played a few outdoor concerts. We started to make real money. Many people work hard and merely make a living. I worked hard and believed in leaving the rest to God. I was not just slated to make a living; I was destined to make a killing.

Chapter 8

A DECISION TO ABORT FURTHER STUDIES

People in the Western Hemisphere might think, "What's the big deal?" If you have money, you can go anywhere in the free world, right? I thought that way as well. I was wrong. People who live in countries whose currency cannot be exchanged in foreign banks and hence is not accepted by the international community cannot just up and visit a foreign country. The host country was to blame as well. Because of international currency laws and regulations, I as an Indian national could not walk into the Reserve Bank of India, a central repository for currency and exchange my rupees for dollars. I had to get clearance and approval from both my native country and the country I chose to visit. The approvals, as I found out, were downright grueling.

The future was going to be wrought with monumental challenges. There were nonstop walls and hurdles all along the way that I would have to scale, overcome, and negotiate.

However, if you believe, God will give you the tools, the ability to apply those tools, and the wisdom you need to overcome all the challenges and hurdles no matter how impossible they may seem. Along the way, he teaches you lessons. Everything always works out. Through it all, God develops your character and gives you the experiences and abilities to tackle things. Finally, one day you will be able to relate to other people's challenges as well, guide them through the pitfalls if they ask for help, not allow them to make excuses, and coach and encourage them to do the same.

Especially in the 1970s in the third world, it did not matter what you had or didn't have. You were not free to do whatever you wanted to do outside your home country. I found out that my counterpart in first- and second-world countries could go anywhere they wanted if they had the money. They also earned 5–10 times the money we earned for the same work. Since I was a third-world human being, I had restrictions. Today, I find it amazing that the liberals want everyone to have everything all the time. Liberals and progressives see struggles as punishment for being born without. I see struggles as a pathway to victory. Liberals and progressives do not follow God Principles at all. In fact, one liberal told me that "God is for the weak. Weak people need God to blame when things don't work out." People who believe in God never blame him for anything whatsoever. If people who believe in God ever blame him for anything, it is in a state of weakness and unbelief that they do so.

Instead of believing in God, liberals and pseudo-intellectuals try to be God with an end goal in mind, to control the masses and the simpletons. They don't understand that in order to trust God to deliver, you have to be extremely strong and not weak. It is easier to not believe in God than it is to believe in God. It is not a God Principle for you to have it all without a struggle and a challenge. Sometimes, a challenge can turn into strife. The reason is simple. Struggle and strife always build character and wisdom if you have the right attitude. If you have the wrong attitude, the same struggle and strife will break you. It is all about your attitude and how you choose to respond that will predicate your outcome. Another liberal, actually a liberal relative of mine, after a Thanksgiving meal, accused me of being "too Christian." What utter stupidity!

If you do not have character and wisdom, you truly lack what it takes to succeed. You know how some people born into a lot of wealth are shallow and could never make it on their own? The reason is that they have not struggled or strived for anything at all. Thus, they lack character. They are vapid and bland with no passion or compassion. Society does not look upon them favorably. On the other hand, I personally know a few billionaires who have very successful children. They did not mollycoddle their children, they did not feather their nests so to speak, and they allowed their children to struggle and then win.

People do not want to accept, understand, and own the God Principle of struggle and strive to be victorious. They cannot fathom why they cannot live large like some do. The only people who can live large are those who truly comprehend and apply the God Principle of struggle in order to be victorious or their parents or grandparents worked that very same God Principle and bequeathed them the finances to live large.

I happened to become extremely responsible and busy at a very young age. I learned to work all waking hours of the day and sleep fast and sound for about four to five hours a day. When you sleep less, you sleep sound. My work ethic and minimal but sound sleep would prove to be invaluable habits throughout my life. When I was in college, my day started at 6:00 a.m. I shaved, showered, and got dressed for breakfast at 7:00 a.m. at the college cafeteria. The cafeteria closed at 7:30 a.m., and if you were late, you got no breakfast. After breakfast, I returned to my dorm room and studied for two hours. I went to class from 10:05 a.m. to 5:10 p.m. five days a week. I was playing music professionally from 7:00 p.m. until 1:00 a.m. three days a week—Thursday, Friday, and Saturday.

I was also captain of my university soccer team. I was on the debate team, and I was a boxer all through high school and college. All that and I have not added the dating thing to the mix, which took an inordinate amount of time as well. I was extremely busy and loved every minute of it. I never complained because no one gave a damn about anyone's plight anyway. They had their own plights to grapple with. I didn't realize it, but

A DECISION TO ABORT FURTHER STUDIES

this was stellar training that would help me throughout my life. My strength was to put in monumental effort to accomplish things and leave the results for God to deliver. He never disappointed.

Each of my professors individually asked me which of the three awesome subjects I had taken in my majors would be my choice for my master's. I said to each of them, "What makes you think I want to do my master's?" They each were taken aback and said I should at the very least get a master's degree and ideally commit and go all the way for a PhD. You see, most people are on a human conveyor belt being groomed to be in the workforce for the best 45 years of their lives. Since the subjects I chose were in high demand, I was encouraged to excel in one of them so I could secure a good middle-class life in the workforce for myself. I laughed and told my professors I didn't think so. At that point, I was making in a month what a PhD professor or scientist was making in a year. I was living the good life, making money, having a blast, and had the ability to even stash a pile. I evaluated the three professors' lifestyles. They drove old used cars or scooters, they lived in crummy houses that they rented, and wore very boring, inexpensive, nondescript clothing. If I had a personal relationship with them, I am sure I would know they were strapped for cash and watched every rupee they spent. That was not the lifestyle I wanted or desired. They literally had nothing I wanted.

All my friends' parents who were businesspeople had everything they seemed to want and more. I came to a very solid conclusion. I decided that the whole brainwash of going to school, getting good grades, working hard, getting a good job, kissing the right anatomy of the right people along the way to the top of the corporate organizational chart was not for me. I have nothing against education, but it was designed as an assembly line for working stiffs. To me, working for someone was twentieth-century slavery. A job is not bad if you have not developed any options and have zero vision. A job is perfect for mediocrity, and mediocrity is just that—mediocre. King Solomon, the wisest human in the history of humankind and blessed by God, said in Proverbs that a person without vision will perish. It was a figure of speech. The word *perish* was used as a metaphor. Solomon was being dramatic to make a point. It is like when you ask someone, "How's business?" they make a face and reply, "Dead." Business is an inanimate intangible; it has no life and hence cannot die. Similarly, perish doesn't mean dead; it means living a life that is devoid of anything but an existence.

Today, *perish* could mean living paycheck to paycheck, never having enough, and always being at the brink of disaster. It could mean racking up too much consumer debt, drinking in bars instead of paying down your college loans, smoking and being broke yet driving a leased BMW. You might say, "How could you be so mean to so many people who are caught up in an unfortunate predicament?" Not really. I am not being mean at all. Nearly everyone has zero debt when they graduate from high school. The predicament, my friend, is self-inflicted. In the free world, people have the ability to make things happen if they choose to have vision and foresight about how they want to ultimately live. Then it takes a plan, a belief in yourself, and discipline to stay the course no matter what. It means deferring gratification for when you are financially strong.

Until you achieve financial strength, you should only afford yourself the bare minimum. It takes deferred gratification to never get into a disadvantaged predicament. It also takes discipline to not spend all the money you make. It takes discipline to buy a used car and not a new one or use public transportation if you can for a while until the time is right when you can buy a car. It takes guts to not lease a car just to impress people. It takes discipline to live in an apartment and save so one day you can put a good chunk down to buy a modest starter home. It takes discipline to not buy a home with the lowest down payment and owe a huge principal and a ton of interest. You must know that all mortgages are front-loaded with interest. The bulk of the interest is paid during the first half of the loan. Initially the interest portion is the major portion of the mortgage payment. It gradually diminishes over the period of the loan. To that, add real estate taxes, insurance, and maintenance costs to the mix. What do you have? You realize you are on the deed, but for all intents and purposes, the lender owns your property until you make the last payment.

In actuality, all you did was plunk down a serious chunk of money for the right to call the house yours. Sure, you have tax deductions and appreciation if there is any. However, if you do not pay the bank, see how long that house belongs to you. The picture changes as fast as a fog can develop on the ocean. This is the normal situation that upper-middle-class, middle-class, and lower-middle-class individuals find themselves in all the time. If this is what you choose, then fine. Just don't expect to live large, and least of all, don't expect the government to equate things. The masses just live life at different levels of broke. Everyone can avoid doing so. Follow the God Principle of struggle followed by victory.

In May 2008, *USA Today* wrote that 57 percent of Americans have less than $1,000 to their name. So it is fair to say that most (57 percent definitely puts things at a level of most) merely exist for the weekend. TGIF (thank God it's Friday) was coined to make things seem lighter and more fun for the working class, when it really is not light, and it is a lot less fun. In free societies, individuals choose the way they live. Our society has lost its sense of discipline. The majority wants the easy way out and everything now. I always say, "Easy does not *pay*." Working for someone else permanently is pure modern slavery in every sense of the word. The most wonderful thing the masses are constantly overlooking is that every single one of us, if we are not mentally challenged, live in a free democratic society and can make a very nice life for ourselves if we truly want to. In order to do that, we must follow some basic principles that are nonnegotiable.

1. Have a stellar attitude. Stop moaning and groaning about inconsequential things as though they mean the world.

A DECISION TO ABORT FURTHER STUDIES

2. Focus on how you want to live as opposed to the work you want to do. Life should always trump work.

3. Have a real game plan, and stick to it no matter what happens, no ifs, ands, or buts. You might have to periodically adjust and tweak the plan. There is a saying: "People don't plan to fail; they fail to plan."

4. Stop postponing and delaying for the right time to come. As soon as the plan is developed, act on it immediately and every single day.

5. Have a work ethic, and work incessantly toward your dreams and goals. Paying bills is critical. Dreams are important. Address the critical, and concurrently never lose sight of the important. Always move forward toward it.

6. Stay with the well-thought-out plan, even when it seems futile and feels like it is not working. All plans take a while to gain traction.

7. Find a mentor.

In a job or career, someone else decides what you are worth, and with that power, they pay you accordingly. Due to that power and the pay scale they assign you, they decide which zip code you can afford to live in. They decide whether you can buy or rent your abode. With that pay and power, they decide whether you can go out to lunch and where you can afford to go to lunch or for that matter whether you can afford to go to lunch or bring your lunch in a brown bag. Due to that power and pay scale, they decide when you go on vacation and where you can afford to go on vacation. All of that is done under the guise of a smile and soft-spoken, civilized speech. Yet it is absolute control, just like slavery was absolute control. I decided against that whole brainwash. I was going to do business. What business? I didn't have a clue, but I was not going to be dictated to. The flip side of not being dictated to is having the discipline to dictate to yourself. A good friend of mine, Dr. Frank Mazzeo, said, "If you don't discipline you, someone else will." He also said, "You can make a million excuses or a million bucks, but you cannot make both." How true these wonderful sayings are.

The Baker's Dozen

The 13 steps to ensure failure:

1. Always moan, groan, and complain about anything and everything.

2. Excuse yourself from taking care of critical and important things.

3. Think you know it all, and be a lousy student.

4. Have a fake sense of accomplishment about yourself.

A DECISION TO ABORT FURTHER STUDIES

5. Postpone things that should and can be done right away.

6. Don't comprehend human behavior, and get tripped up constantly by people and their behavior.

7. Blame someone else for your mistakes, and don't take responsibility for your actions.

8. Don't be brutally harsh with yourself when you are wrong.

9. Don't comprehend that success, like most things, has a ratio.

10. Don't respect the time it takes to get exactly what you want.

11. Be too caught up with what you like to do as opposed to what you need to do to accomplish your goal.

12. Talk and think negatively about the people you work with.

13. Compare yourself to others for the wrong reasons.

Chapter 9

LEADING UP TO LEAVING INDIA

Just before I tasted some success in the music business, I had decided to visit the USA to check it out. According to conventional wisdom, I was putting the cart before the horse. There was no reason for a kid like me from middle-class India to visit the USA. However, I was following a four-step process without knowing it.

This was the process:

Step One: Define your dream.

Step Two: Commit to it.

Step Three: Develop a God-provided plan, and put it in action.

Step Four: Work hard without negotiating the time, energy, or financial or emotional price you will have to pay.

As a musician, I often think in terms of songs. In this case, I think of two wildly successful songs with crummy messages. The first is "Que Sera Sera" made famous by Doris Day who performed it in Alfred Hitchcock's 1956 movie *The Man Who Knew Too Much*. The song promotes compromise and mediocrity, implying that we're all victims of circumstance and that we should be satisfied with a preordained life. It negates free will, the fact that God allows us to develop our lives based on our desires and wishes, be they good, bad, or ugly. Life is never "whatever will be will be." We have total control of what we can achieve if we follow the principles I mentioned in the four-step process above. The real message should be a 10-word set of two-letter words: "If it is to be, it is up to me." The second song that comes to mind is "Two Out of Three Ain't Bad," a mega hit performed by Meat Loaf on his 1977 album *Bat Out of Hell*. Again, the lyrics push compromise and settling for less. They should say, "I won't settle for two out of three. I don't stop until I achieve three out of three." The song I recommend is "I Want It All" by the inimitable rock band Queen. That's a rock anthem worth following.

Uncalled for challenges arise when we settle, when we leave out a single step or multiple key ingredients. I definitely had a dream, I definitely knew how to commit, and I definitely knew how to work hard. Here is where faith in God kicks in. Without having a plan, I spoke of my dream as though everything was in place. If you believe in God and what you want is honorable, he fills in the blanks by using people around you to guide and assist you along the way. This is another God Principle. Take note: Even secular people can apply a God Principle and achieve success. Because God gave us free will and never reneges on his word, even criminals can implement the God Principle with success. The only difference is that they apply it to a criminal deed rather than righteous deeds. Principles are intangible instruments that can be used for good or for bad, depending on the user. A car with a drunk or enraged person behind the wheel can kill, maim, or injure, while a sober person can accomplish a fairly simple task—driving from point A to point B. In and of itself, a car is a harmless piece of sheet metal with some critical enhancements. So also is a principle only as good or bad as the person applying it. God filled in my blanks because I believed. He does not fill in the blanks with secular people. Secular nonbelievers will have to put all things in place by themselves and implement them properly in order to win. Their win would have been much bigger and more rewarding with God's help.

God used Ajay and his seemingly cockamamie idea of entering that Simla contest to help me realize my dream. Because I was dedicated, I learned the skills to achieve that dream. God worked on my behalf, and he will work on yours as well if you only believe in him and truly allow him to help you. All I had to do was believe in him and then use the wonderful brain he endowed me with and keep working. The plan came to fruition through the band and winning the contests. I worked incessantly, and God did the rest. He walked me through it all, regardless of how impossible it may have seemed. And, boy, did it seem impossible!

Chapter 10

BECOMING UNRELATABLE IN MY COMMUNITY

When I decided to visit the USA, I started openly voicing my plans to friends and family if they asked. It's commonplace for people to ask you what you do for a living or what you will do after graduating from college. Most of my friends, relatives, and acquaintances were middle class and therefore all about working a job, looking for work, or getting a degree to obtain better work. Life was all about the job. Don't get me wrong, there is nothing wrong with a job. However, a typical job did not sit well for someone like me who never wanted to be controlled by another person. So with no money, no real game plan, a huge dream, and a strong belief in God, I answered the commonplace question often posed to me like this: "I plan to visit the USA to check it out." Come to think of it, that was one heck of a stretch, to say the least.

Now I need to deviate a bit to give you a little background on India in the late 1960s. Back then, 99.9 percent of the people in India never traveled abroad. It was not that they did not want to. It was that the average working Indian made about $75 per month, making it impossible to do so. In fact, people were put on a very high social pedestal if they had ever traveled anywhere abroad. And of all the places in the world, if one was fortunate enough to go to the USA, they reached the epitome of that social pedestal. So whenever I expressed my plans to visit the USA, people were intrigued. They would perk up and show either immense interest or utter disdain. Some would drill down further and ask how I managed to get a job or admission to a graduate program in the USA while I was still in an undergrad program. I must note that you literally had to be brilliant to qualify for a job or a graduate studies program abroad. Most Indians could not afford to underwrite their child's college tuition and living expenses in India, let alone cover the astronomical cost overseas. To get admission to a graduate study program, you had to be smart enough to qualify for a 100 percent scholarship with a job of some kind that had a stipend to cover personal expenses—something one could definitely not do remotely from India, especially since there was no Internet or satellite TV. A solid middle-class family of four was fortunate to make 1,200–1,500 rupees ($160–$200) per month.

People were flabbergasted with my answer and

wondered how I could possibly afford something so financially out of reach. When I told them that I was just going to the US to decide if I liked it enough to live there, they were bewildered.

"You surely must have something lined up, right?" they asked me. "You could not possibly go all the way to the other end of the world on a lark to see if you want to live there. And of all the places, America? It is a very expensive place."

I would smile and repeat, "I plan to visit and see if I like it."

Some would say, "You can't be serious!"

But I would nod, smile, and say, "That is what I intend to do."

They wondered what was wrong with me. On the surface, I seemed pretty normal, even moderately intelligent. Yet I had to be either delusional or stark raving mad. No one in my social strata spoke as I did. If I spoke to military officers who worked with my dad, they told my father, "Do you know what your son is telling everyone?"

I put my dad in a tough spot, but as a senior army officer, he was never at a loss for words. He would say, "My son is a very sharp boy; he will figure things out. He definitely has the right to explore all his options." They would then be totally flabbergasted all over again because fathers were supposed to put some sense into their sons and rein them in when they talked nonsense.

My plans became a huge problem for me, but I never stopped expressing them, and my parents never sat me down and said, "Son, have you really thought things through?" or "You might want to rethink what you say to people."

Friends can be vicious, obnoxious, and downright brutal. If I went to the college cafeteria, I often heard, "Here comes the American who's never been to the USA," or "Here comes the man with no plan." I learned in those three years leading up to my departure that when you decide to take the high road, when you do things that are not considered the norm, you will be ridiculed by almost everyone. In fact, when I was in college, a Catholic priest who was a faculty member told me in a public setting that I was most likely to fail. I was appalled by this amazing negativity spoken publicly—and by a priest no less. It mattered not that I had good grades, that I was a good athlete, or that I was extremely popular. All that mattered was that I was not following a socially acceptable plan. According to societal norms, I didn't fit into their meter of judgment. I was shooting from the hip, and that, indeed, was not the proper, responsible way for an educated person to behave.

The more people put me down, whether in jest or seriously, the tougher I grew mentally and emotionally. They made me adamant about this America thing. So when Ajay made that whole Modern Bookstore contest happen, he did not know that he was instrumental in a bigger plan. And strangely enough, neither did I. It was part of a plan that would provide the finances for my visit to the USA. I was so unaware of the contest's potential that I fought Ajay from the start quite a bit. However,

God was working his plan for me through the people around me. The naysayers were toughening me up for what was to come. I learned to sleep four to five hours a night, worked hard all day, and didn't drop the ball on multiple fronts. Ajay put the beginnings of the plan in place, and it was my duty not to negotiate the price of my success.

I say this all the time: You can negotiate the price of a pair of shoes; you can negotiate the price of an automobile. You can negotiate the price of a house, but you cannot negotiate the price of your success or a relationship or a spiritual walk with God. And believe me, if you want the big picture to materialize, you will pay an inordinate price for the intangibles I just mentioned.

I must also mention this: If you think the word *price* pertains only to money, you have much to learn. You need to think and think hard about the true price we all have to pay for everything we want and achieve. Price is your intellectual input, your ability to think, analyze, and make decisions. Price is your emotional input, your ability to be strong against all odds, not waver in the midst of adversity, and have an upbeat attitude no matter what transpires. Price is your physical input, your ability to devote long, sometimes bleak hours every day without complaining. Price is your spiritual input, your innate ability to believe that your vision will materialize into reality because God is on your side to bless you beyond your comprehension. Price is your financial input, your ability to invest and not think that every darn thing is an expense. Finally, price is your faith input, your ability to see things through. Once you decide to do something and believe in God's ability to bless and shower you with his grace, the path to achievement, though a monumental effort, is nothing short of a miracle.

I was excited and nervous beyond belief. I was preparing to actually leave the country I was born in. I was going to a faraway land that my grandfather had so fondly told me about more than a decade ago, a land I had only experienced in books, magazines, and movies. The movies depicted most everyone with a car and living in nice houses with all the modern amenities known to humanity. In America, everyone had refrigerators, TVs, radios, and beautiful furnishings. It seemed they all lived better than the rich lived in India. And when I got to America, it was all true. The poor in the US had more than the rich in India in terms of modern amenities and comfortable living.

I watched the movie *Giant,* starring Rock Hudson, James Dean, and Elizabeth Taylor. Wow! What an amazing story about making it in the oil business! Even that movie was meant to inspire me. I needed to never give up and believe that God would make it happen if I thought right, committed, and acted on it. However, I soon realized that movie stars, rock-and-roll musicians, athletes, and politicians were not to be idolized. The two guys in *Giant* were definitely not my kind of guys, even though they were handsome as all heck.

Here is a very silly and immature thing I did when I was 15—something I should never have done. I started smoking, all because of James Dean. He smoked like he meant it, and I thought if I smoked like him, I would definitely be a chick magnet. That was a huge mistake. I did, however, kick the habit cold 10 years later, and I am glad I did.

I saw all the Elvis, Rock Hudson, and Doris Day movies. I watched *Woodstock*, the movie. I was singing all the international hits by the Beatles, the Bee Gees, Cream, Jimi Hendrix, Credence Clearwater Revival, Simon & Garfunkel, the Rolling Stones, Otis Redding, Sam Cooke, and more. Now I was going to the land that made these megastars famous. No one—no entity, company, or organization—was anything at all until they made it in America. And I was going to that land. Wow!

Since I had never left the shores of India, I started to think about all the what-ifs. Even though what-ifs are an essential part of planning, they tend to be top-heavy on the negative and can drive you nuts. I spent all my waking hours being outwardly noisy, jovial, happy, and the usually spontaneous person that I am. However, internally my mind was a blur. As an army brat, I was not averse to moving. My dad was transferred every three years or so to a different base. But my travel experience was only domestic. The music business upped the ante on travel quite a bit, but it was still only domestic travel. Now, after almost three years of telling everyone I was going to the USA, it was actually going to happen.

Another biblical principle was in play here: Speak it into existence. This principle became a powerful reality in my life. In Genesis, God spoke the universe and all that is in it into existence. He made us in his image.

Image in the biblical sense is more than just visual. We have been endowed with a lot of God's traits. One of them is that we also can speak things into existence. Secular people often do not understand this principle but rather circle the issue. I had spoken visiting America into existence when logic would have dictated otherwise. I had absolutely nothing at all to make my visit to America a possibility, never mind a reality. I was going to make my first international trip, and it was not to Nepal or Tibet or Ceylon (now known as Sri Lanka). I was going on an intercontinental trip halfway around the world to the ultimate destination—the USA. When it was 9:00 a.m. in India, it was 10:30 p.m. the day before on the East Coast of the USA. Wow! That was a 10.5-hour time difference from almost halfway around the world. I was going to New York. It was no longer just an answer to a question. It was about to be a reality.

Chapter 11

THE DEAL THAT STARTED IT ALL

In 1969, I made a handshake deal with a trusted family friend, Suresh Shukla. He was touted by the family as a successful New York businessman. He happened to be visiting India with his French wife, Michelle, and their newborn son. I told him I was going to the US, and if I decided to stay, I would very much like to go into business with him in New York. He was 36, and I was not quite 19, almost half his age. He said sure, but I found out later that he never took me seriously. Just like everyone else, he thought I was talking through my hat. Like everyone else, he thought, "How on earth would the son of an Indian army officer have the resources to come to the USA, never mind get into business?" When I had my ticket and visa in hand, I called him long distance from India and told him I was arriving at 7:00 p.m. on January 13, 1971, on an Air India flight from Bombay to New York City. I asked him if he could pick me up at the John F. Kennedy Airport. He said he would be there. I was fired up. Just saying the words "can you pick me up at the John F. Kennedy Airport" was exhilarating.

Christmas and New Year's Day in India were full of parties and goodbyes. People were flabbergasted as to how I had finally pulled things together to go to New York. They knew I was a popular front man with a successful band, but I was just an undergrad student, for crying out loud. It just wasn't possible. What if I came back to India? I would have burned through a fortune for pretty much nothing. However, I had a powerful desire to fulfill a dream. Though people were sure I was making a gigantic mistake, I was sure I was spot on.

Now it was my turn to enjoy the confusion I'd created in their small minds. You see, I had one thing going for me. I believed that if I wanted to, I could do pretty much anything, and the size of the project was never going to be an issue. Since there was no regulation on thought, I simply thought big. Unfortunately, it was to the chagrin of the people in my circle of influence. That sort of thinking was rubbish according to the strata of society I lived in. Well, I am sorry to say, I was right, and they were wrong. I was loving every minute of the unsaid I-told-you-so moments I enjoyed. Don't forget, these were the same people who had been ridiculing me for about the past three years. Success is the sweetest revenge.

Finally, the day came. On January 12, 1971, I took a

THE DEAL THAT STARTED IT ALL

short, 90-minute domestic Indian Airline flight at 6:00 p.m. to Bombay. I had an 11:30 p.m. Air India Boeing 747 flight to New York City. Talk about being fired up and nervous all at once. I had only read about the Boeing 747. It was a brand-new plane, and very few airlines had even bought one. Air India bought two to use exclusively for the Bombay–New York–Bombay route. There was only one flight out every day. Today, you can catch a direct flight from New Delhi or Mumbai to Newark, New Jersey, and in 16 hours and 45 minutes, you reach your destination. The flight I took in 1971 took more than 31 hours. It stopped at many places—Tehran, Bahrain, Beirut, Istanbul, London, and finally New York City. I must admit, I enjoyed every minute of that arduous journey.

My oldest sister, Cynthia, worked in Bombay and was dating a man my age, six years younger than she was. It was a very avant-garde thing to do for an Indian woman. It must be noted that dating was typically restricted, and arranged marriages were and still are the norm. There was a large entourage that saw me off in New Delhi, and when I landed in Bombay, Cynthia and her boyfriend met me at the airport. We had dinner and talked for about an hour before my flight was called. We hugged and said our goodbyes, and then I boarded the huge Boeing 747 for the US. Man, oh, man, that was something! It was going to be spectacular for that behemoth craft to get airborne. Remember, one of my three majors was physics, and I found it amazing that this tonnage actually flew. It was almost 1:00 a.m. when we leveled off around 34,000 feet and they served us dinner. I had already eaten a whole meal at 9:00 p.m. with my sister and her boyfriend, but with the excitement and high adrenaline, I ate again at about 1:00 a.m. IST (Indian Standard Time). I was getting used to the whole process and settling in nicely. I listened to piped-in music through headphones provided by the cabin crew. I had never experienced music piped in via a couple of small holes on an armrest before, and in about 20 minutes, the state-of-the-art headphones started hurting my ears. Thank the good Lord for the advancement of technology; things have certainly improved by leaps and bounds. As soon as the seat belt sign went off, everyone and their offspring lit up a cigarette. It was crazy, but that was the old normal. About 45 minutes after take-off, the captain came over the intercom to announce that we were leaving Indian airspace. I froze!

When I was about 13 years old during summer vacation, my mom, sisters, and I were hanging out at home in the drawing room (living room in British English). We heard the familiar sound of my father's army Jeep drive up our driveway. Dad was such a cool guy. Later on, when I saw the movie *Patton*, I realized that my dad was a Patton fan. His whole demeanor was like General George Patton. He had a no-holds-barred attitude in pretty much everything he did. He was a very upbeat guy who could turn on a dime and become a vicious killer as he was trained to be. The only time he was always gentle and mild mannered was with my mom. In my business seminars, I tell everyone, "My

THE DEAL THAT STARTED IT ALL

father commanded troops, and my mother commanded my father." He would ride that olive-green, military-issue, open-air Willys Jeep with the windscreen folded down onto the hood, one foot on the outside running board and one hand holding the upper end of the door frame. My father had an air of authority that I thought was simply awesome.

On that day, Dad brought home the new fire chief (Chief Gupta) from the military base. He was a big man with a big personality. Dad introduced him to my mom and us kids, and my mother was not happy. She did not like surprises, and my dad had not prepared her for this visit—a big no-no. Needless to say, my mother was polite but not her outgoing self. That was her passive way of showing her displeasure. My dad sensed her frustration and did most of the talking. The cook served tea and snacks per my mother's instructions. I was happy since I was always ready as a growing male for an opportunity to eat some good stuff.

After we ate, Dad said, "Chief Gupta's father is an acclaimed palmist. He's read the palms of some famous people—the chief minister of the state, a couple of famous movie stars, and others. The chief learned this age-old science from his father, and he has turned out to be a pretty good palmist himself."

The chief was visibly proud that the big boss was promoting him, and he turned to my mother. "Madam, kindly let me see your good hand," he said and extended his own.

My mother said, "No, that's all right." As Christians,

we did not believe in palmistry or other things such as astrology, numerology, feng shui, and so forth.

The chief assumed that Mom hesitated because she did not want any negative predictions. So he said, "Madam, I promise I will not say anything negative to you."

She said, "Oh no, that is perfectly all right."

But he insisted, and to avoid being rude, my mom reluctantly extended her right hand.

He said, "No, Madam, your left hand, please." Looking at her left palm, he said, "Madam, this is very interesting. This line shows that in the future, you will go abroad so often that it will be like going from your living room to your bedroom."

My mother laughed out loud and thanked him for his words. Inside, she thought this fool was trying to curry favor by saying outlandish things to make me feel good.

I ran from my chair and thrust my left hand in front of the chief. I asked excitedly, "What does my hand say?"

He said, "Baba [young boy in the vernacular], your hand is not developed yet. Moreover, for males, it is the right hand."

I thrust my right hand and pressed him. "C'mon. Something has developed."

He looked at my right hand, and his face fell. He blurted out, "Baba, you will have more than one marriage, and you will not die in India. You will have a very hectic life, but through all your challenges, you will never lack for money."

I thought, *"Hmm! That was quite a bit for an undeveloped hand."*

THE DEAL THAT STARTED IT ALL

My mother threw her head back and laughed heartily. She said, "Son, don't ever leave this country, and you will live forever."

Everybody laughed. Chief Gupta was so completely outlandish in his predictions that we never paid it any mind. That was more than nine years before I boarded that flight. When I heard the pilot announce over the intercom that we were leaving Indian airspace, I remembered this whole episode vividly. I hoped this huge plane would not fall out of the sky and fulfill Chief Gupta's predictions. Today, I count three predictions that Chief Gupta made that have already come true. For the last 19 years of my mom's life, she traveled extensively to and from India to the US since I lived here. I was married more than once, and I have had a very wonderfully hectic life with monumental hardships along the way. Through it all, I was in many financially challenging times, but I never personally lacked for money. The last prediction is tracking to be true as well, considering I live in the US. Even though I travel to India regularly, it is highly unlikely that I will die in any place but the US.

Chapter 12

NEW YORK, NEW YORK

When my flight finally landed at New York's JFK Airport, I claimed my bags and went through customs, as is required. It was around 8:30 p.m. EST (Eastern Standard Time). Wearing tropical wool slacks, a button-down cotton shirt, and my favorite military camouflage jacket, I exited the international security area and entered the main terminal to find Suresh. I looked and looked, but there was no Suresh. I was not happy. Here I was far away from home in an unfamiliar country, and the one guy I trusted and put all my faith in who had promised to meet me at JFK was nowhere to be found. It was a very disconcerting feeling for a 20-year-old who had never traveled outside India.

Deciding to catch a cab and go to his apartment, I headed to the exit and stepped on the rubber mat in front of the doors. The double doors swung open without my ever touching them. I dropped my bag, dazed. Who opened the door?

"What's the holdup? Let's go!" said a gruff voice behind me. I moved forward and realized that the mat had a switch mechanism that opened the door. I had never experienced that before. It shows you how naïve I was about pretty much everything.

When I stepped outside, I was in for another shock. It was only 9 degrees Fahrenheit, much colder than I'd ever experienced. My camouflage jacket, cotton shirt, and tropical wool slacks were almost useless. Shivering visibly, I jumped into the first cab I saw.

"Where to?" the cab driver asked.

"Go to 32 Gramercy Park South, on the corner of 20th and 3rd," I said with confidence, not knowing how truly New Yorker I sounded. I liked Suresh's address because it had a ring to it. I used to practice saying it when I was in India so one day it would flow out of my mouth as if I were a local. And it did.

The cabby took me there, and I asked him to wait in case my friend was not home and I would need to check into a hotel. Inside the building, a man at a counter enclosed in glass asked, "Can I help you?"

"I am here to visit Mr. Suresh Shukla in apartment 16E," I said.

"Please wait." He lifted a phone and said, "Hello, Mr. Shukla." He listened a moment and then asked me my name. I gave it to him. He said in the phone, "Leo Jesudian is here to see you, Sir." Then he hung up and said, "You can go up. The elevators are on your left."

I liked that term, *elevator*. Back home, we called them lifts. I went out, paid the cabby, and proceeded to the elevators. I went up to apartment 16E where Suresh and his wife greeted me as if they hadn't been scheduled to pick me up. He later made a feeble excuse about a meeting that went on forever. It is funny how excuses only satisfy the ones making them and no one else. I was half his age and would never have left someone stranded at the airport if I had made a commitment to pick them up, especially if it were their first trip abroad and the person was only 20 years old. I would have cut the meeting short. What good is anyone if their word means nothing?

Something strange happened that night. Suresh was a no-show at the airport, and I was grossly underprepared for the ultra-cold night. It should have made me concerned about moving to the US. It should have turned me off. However, for some reason, the opposite happened. I felt this warm feeling deep inside; I felt like I was home. How absurd is that? I decided on that first night to live in the USA. I didn't have a clue how that was going to play out, but I made the decision.

The next day, Suresh and I talked about going into business together. He asked how much money I had, and I said, "In dollars, about $10,000." After some serious discussions, we concluded that for $10,000, he would make me a 50 percent partner in the store he had just opened on Sheridan Square in the West Village in Manhattan. The address was 122½ 7th Avenue South on the corner of 10th and 7th. I was in the heart of it all. Village Cigars was half a block south of me. A block north was the world-famous jazz club Village Vanguard where Charlie Mingus and Charles Lloyd played live all the time. The Ninth Circle, another great night spot with live music, was two blocks across town. In front of me was Your Father's Moustache, a hugely popular live Dixieland jazz club. Four blocks from me was the Village Gate where Jimi Hendrix used to sit and jam when he first started out.

I was in heaven, despite the fact that I worked nonstop 14 hours a day, 7 days a week, 365 days a year. I didn't immigrate to the US, the land of opportunity, to do the minimum to get by. I came to be an American and realize my dreams. I was going to excel. I was going to make it and be someone. My store hours were 10:00 a.m. to midnight every day, including Christmas, Easter, Independence Day, and New Year's Day. One awful fallout was that I didn't go to church for a few years. However, my belief and trust in God never waned. In fact, many things happened that strengthened my faith in God.

Even though my social life started at midnight, I made sure it stayed active. All my dates were at midnight. If any woman had a problem with that, I would just not date her. I had one shot to make it, and I was going to take it. I was going to be successful, no excuses. No man, woman, organization, corporation, government, or circumstance was going to get in my way. I had paid too high a price financially, emotionally, physically, and intellectually to consider failure as an option. Plus, I had God on my side. How could I lose?

Though I had never sold a tangible thing in my life, I had become astute at selling intangibles. I sold good times to get every contract in the music business. I sold myself in a winning debate with the Consul General of the US Embassy in New Delhi. He was obliged to give me the visa because God literally put words in my mouth to defeat any point he raised. Through the years, I realized that people who sell intangibles far exceed in their ability to sell than those who sell tangibles. It is much easier to sell a car than to sell insurance. It is much easier to sell a house than to sell consulting services. Please don't miss the point. It is always hard to become a professional and sell anything. Some things are just easier (not easy) to sell than others.

The first two days I was at the store in West Village I said nothing. I just observed, asked questions, and spoke when I was spoken to. I was listening and learning. In a matter of weeks, I realized that I needed to make people feel comfortable in order for them to even consider buying anything. How would I do that? I would ask fun questions, compliment anything real about them, and listen. Most people are starved for attention. If you listen and give them your undivided attention, they will like you and feel comfortable in your company.

Within two months, I became skilled at making and closing sales. The most important thing I learned was that asking someone if they needed help was just like asking someone in a bar if they wanted to be picked up. Both questions are met with hostility, though most shoppers usually need some help and most bar-goers usually want to be picked up. So unfortunately, being direct doesn't work.

The key to selling is also the key to dating. You talk about everything in Christendom except the issue on everyone's mind. I was an ace at dating, so I became an ace at selling. Becoming good at anything requires a willingness to suck at it long enough to make progress. Once you make progress, you eventually become good.

The first month was a disaster. Not only was it cold in January, but I couldn't make sales. I will never forget my first day in business. I took in $37.50 in 14 hours. I was petrified. It was cold and nasty, and business stank. The revenue for the month of January was about $5,000, and my rent was $900. The electricity, heat, phone, and other operating expenses, along with the cost of goods, made it a very gloomy month. To top it off, my partner never came to work and never assisted with anything after the first week or so. He feigned being busy with other stuff, but he made it a point to be there every night before we closed to take all the cash in the drawer, leaving only the checks and charges as operating capital for me to work with. That made it extremely difficult to make ends meet, but I was the junior person, so I shut up and managed.

March was a wee bit better, and the weather broke. April was a breath of fresh air. The checks and charges together made for real working capital. However, my partner was getting on my nerves. He was stealing all the cash. Every night, he took every dollar except the starting cash in the register. I remained quiet. We had a great summer, and I managed to build up the inventory, pay all the vendors, cover the overhead, and even afford a salesperson I had hired to work 40 hours a week. I had not only become independent, I had created a job.

My lawyer said that was great for my application for permanent residency since the government would look at me as a person who didn't come to the US to take a job. I not only created my own employment but I had created an additional job. My partner and his French wife, Michelle, decided to visit India that fall. They bought their tickets by writing a check from the business account and then left for a month. I was not happy that they spent the money from the company account for a personal vacation after stealing all the cash every day. However, that month, I had a blast. I found out how good it was to have all the daily receipts to work with. How crazy was that? I managed to have a balance of $5,000 in the operating account and was current with all the bills.

It was nuts, but my fantasy was to have all the money that came into the business to run it. I realized how stupid that fantasy was and decided to have a heart-to-heart with Suresh when he returned. When he returned, I kept postponing the talk for two reasons. One, business was brisk, and I was busy 14 hours a day. Two, the real reason was that I was not in the mood to have a sticky conversation. Things were looking up, and I decided to talk to him when things quieted down a bit. It was a total cop-out. I learned later to nip things in the bud after that experience.

In early October, Suresh came into the store excited and said there was a 1,000-square-foot corner store on

62nd and Lexington, two blocks north of Bloomingdale's. He wanted us to rent it, but he said we needed $10,000 extra. I said we had that in the account and could maybe squeeze through if we didn't raid the till every night. He said we needed $6,000 for the lease alone, and then there were legal fees along with the cost of a build-out and a pull-down metal grate to go down over the plate-glass windows at night, which was going to cost $3,000. We really needed $10,000 more than we had. I told him that if we could not afford it, we should just wait and do things when we could. Salivating over something we couldn't afford was counterproductive.

Suresh and his wife, Michelle, suggested that my girlfriend, Karen, who was a registered nurse at the ICU in Bellevue Hospital, might be able to front us the money. They said we only needed it for about 90 days or so. I said I would not have it. While we were talking, Karen came into the store as she usually did every day after she finished working. They told her about the store, and she asked when we were going to open it.

Suresh said, "Leo and I are short $10,000, so it is going to be tough."

She offered to help, but I said no, that it would not be necessary.

Karen insisted, and it was game on. We opened the store on November 10, and by December 31, we had taken in more than $100,000. That was monumental for 1971. We were on a roll. The store in the village was doing great, and now this store on the Upper East Side was hotter than a pistol. I made sure Karen was paid off with interest, and I took her on an upscale night out to thank her.

With two stores doing great, we went into the New Year with gusto. In 1972, we took in about $800,000 for the two stores. Everything was fantastic. I moved into a two-bedroom penthouse apartment in a sexy NYC building on the Upper East Side and was enjoying the good life. I now had five employees and a solid business.

The downside was that Suresh was still stealing cash from the register every night. It was really getting out of hand. A brand new Cadillac Sedan DeVille cost $7,200 in 1972, and my partner used to walk around with $4,000–$5,000 in his pocket like a big shot. However, there was so much cash flow that I didn't have a problem operating the business. We both took a hefty salary in 1972. We ate out and entertained with corporate credit cards, and life was good. However, the 50-50 partnership needed to be addressed. Suresh was stealing gobs of cash every night.

On New Year's Eve in 1972, we were celebrating with champagne and some awesome food when Suresh asked to talk to me. I said, "Sure, we really need to talk." He proceeded to tell me how much I had grown as a businessman and how proud he was of me. Sure, I only did everything all the time and wholly ran a very successful retail business that made us fantastic livings while he stole all the cash. Finally, he said, "I have taught you everything I know."

I laughed. He never taught me anything. He never took me under his wing as I thought he would. All he did was steal money and act like a big shot. Oh! I stand corrected. He did teach me something. He taught me what not to do, that's for sure.

Then he dropped the bomb. "Leo, I am going to give you back 100 percent of the money you gave me. I now am confident you will be a very successful businessman. It is time for you to spread your wings and fly on your own."

I was shocked. "What do you mean you will give me back 100 percent of the money I gave you? I am a 50 percent partner, and our company is worth one year's gross or six years' net. At the low end, that would make my share $300,000, and at the high end, it would be $400,000."

Both Suresh and Michelle laughed. "You really think you are a 50 percent partner when we were the ones that made it all happen? If it were not for us, you would not be living in the US."

"Part of what you say is true," I said. "However, I have made things very good for you as well. You never even made the business happen. I made it all happen. I am the one who worked 100 hours a week for the past two years, and all you two did was steal the money from the cash register every night. I was the one who built our reserves, which, along with Karen's short-term loan, made the Lexington Avenue store possible."

They both rolled their eyes and smiled. "You aren't serious. We really think you should move on since now it is apparent that our whole outlook on business is not the same."

I agreed with them wholeheartedly on that count. I told them that their outlook was to rape the business every night, and mine was to build a solid asset. I told them they were making a grave mistake. "If you would not be so greedy in the short term and steal all the cash, we could open 100 stores over the next five years in all the key cities in the US and birth a real robust business," I said.

But they wanted me out, and I had nothing on paper to fight it. I also did not have a green card yet. My papers were in process. It was a naïve handshake deal that I made that cold day in January 1971. I did not have a legal leg to stand on. I was out.

Since I had no debt and no credit cards of my own, I could not even buy a car. I had worked so hard, was myopic in my work life, and had neglected everything else. I realized I was a money-making machine for my partner. The stupidest thing was that he and his lovely wife were killing the goose that laid the golden egg. I was incensed, not because I lost almost $400,000 and had worked all hours of the day to develop a real business, but because it was yanked from me at the age of 22. I was disgusted at how naïve I was and that I was taken for a total fool. It was not a good feeling at all and a very heavy lesson to learn. But when God teaches you, the best thing to do is shut up and learn. In the Bible, Job had it much worse, so I would be patient and do all over again what I had become so good at—business development. Except this time, I was going to do it for me. It's not over until the fat lady sings, goes the old adage.

And when does the fat lady sing? When you die. I wasn't dead yet.

I had broken up with Karen a few months earlier after she accused me of being a fake. She accused me of acting like I owned the city when I didn't have a pot to pee in. She did not understand the God Principle of speaking something into existence. I should never have borrowed the money from her. She felt superior from that time forward, and our relationship deteriorated. She lost respect for me. Even though I was not in love with her, her words stung, and I was thrown for a loop emotionally for a couple of weeks. Karen was 27, had a responsible job, and was a nice person, so I respected her.

Two weeks after Karen and I broke up, I went on a woman rampage and dated scores of women without really caring for any of them. I knew it was a shallow thing to do, but I was in no mood to be deep. All the women I dated had to meet three criteria: They had to be good looking, clean, and able to hold a decent conversation. That was it. I was going to ride and break the horse that threw me. I was going to win.

After about two months of pure debauchery, I did some self-evaluation and became disgusted with my behavior. That was when I met a brunette named Lisa. She was a 1970s version of Greta Garbo. We dated, and before long she was living with me. When she found out about my split from Suresh, she was deeply shaken. I thought that was sweet of her.

Meanwhile, I was looking at a store on 72nd Street between Madison and 5th. While I was negotiating the lease, I talked to my suppliers about stocking the store and garnering the required inventory. To my surprise, Suresh had already talked to all of them and told them not to supply me. "Suresh told us that if we supply you in New York City, he will not buy goods from us anymore," they said. "So we seriously think you should leave the city and open a store where you don't compete with Suresh. That way, we can supply you and not lose the two-store account we have with Suresh in New York City."

I was beside myself. First, Karen called me a fake, and then Suresh pulled the rug from under my feet financially. Now I was being stonewalled right out of the city by the very businesses I'd paid on time for the past two years, even though Suresh stole all the cash every day and made operating the business challenging.

Chapter 13

MOVE TO BOSTON

When Lisa heard what was happening, she told me, "Don't worry. We can go to Boston."
"What's in Boston?" I asked her.
She said it was a great city, young and very intellectual with more than a quarter of a million university students, the most in the world in one city. I didn't need too much convincing. I rented a car, and we drove to Boston to explore the possibilities. We checked into the Treadway Inn in Harvard Square and spent the next two days looking around. Within a four-day spell, I rented a store in Harvard Square in the Garage, a hip new indoor mall owned by the Wasserman Group. Max Wasserman and his son Peter Wasserman met with me, and I rented store no. 13 in the Garage at 36 Boylston Street, Cambridge, Massachusetts.

I came to the US on January 13, 1971, and now,

for the first time, I was in business for myself with no partners and in store no. 13. Nice! And people have a problem with the number 13 being unlucky. All over the world, people have trouble numbering the 13th floor in buildings. The elevators in all high-rises skip floor 13 and go to 14. How ridiculous is that? Big-time developers are playing games with adults based on nothing but a myth and superstition. That shows you how ridiculous humans can be. The number 13 turned out to be a good number for me if you are into those kinds of things. I am not into those kinds of things, but it was an interesting fact.

I returned to New York City, and all the suppliers were happy to see and support me when I told them I rented a store in Cambridge, Massachusetts. Now I needed a car. Since I had no personal debt and still did not have a Social Security number, I was fresh out of luck when I went to buy because I could not get a loan. I asked Suresh if I could take the company car the stores owned in New York. I would assume the monthly payments for the balance of the 18 remaining months, and he could get a new car. He stuck it to me again. He said he would deduct the price of the car from the money he owed me, and I could have it. I asked him how much. He said in a matter-of-fact voice the price the company paid.

"C'mon, be reasonable," I said. "It's 18 months old. You cannot possibly sell me a used car for the full list price of a brand new car. I can pay you the full Blue Book value for the car."

He smiled and said, "Take it or leave it."

MOVE TO BOSTON

I had no other choice since I needed a car to do business in Boston and didn't qualify for a loan. I needed a car to commute every week from Boston to New York to replenish my store with inventory, so I took the darned used car for the full price. Now I had little or nothing left after putting a down payment on the store in Cambridge, putting first and last month's rent down for an apartment, spending money to explore, and paying cash for that 18-month-old used burgundy and white 1971 Volkswagen van. Anyway, I had to make lemonade from a lemon relationship I had initiated.

I opened my store in Cambridge on July 5, 1973. It was déjà vu of 1971. There was scant inventory at first because of the lack of funds, but even with all the ups and downs, by December 31, the store was fully stocked with inventory that was paid for. I had paid all my bills and had a stash of about $8,000 cash on hand. In March 1974, I bought a new Mazda RX 3, the one with the German Wankel engine. It was a blast—a station wagon that outran a BMW 2002 with ease.

Once again, with perseverance and God's blessings, I was on an upward path, rising out of a difficult predicament. I worked long hours, except this time it was 100 percent my business. There was more good news to follow. In early March, a few days after I bought my new car, I got a letter from the INS (Immigration and Naturalization Service, now known as Immigration and Customs Enforcement (ICE)). It said I was granted an interview for my green card later that month. I called my immigration attorney, Sy Rosenbloom, in New York and asked him if it meant what I thought it meant.

With great gusto, he answered, "Yes! You are all set, Leo. Congratulations! You have been approved for a green card." I hung up the phone and was flying high all over again. How wonderful was this? My hard work, tenacity, perseverance, and, most of all, complete belief in my God was producing fruit all over again. I had withstood some hard times, and now the famine was over. It had rained, and now there was abundance. I was officially going to be confirmed as a resident of the United States of America. I looked up, raised my hands, and shouted out loud, "Thank you, Lord!" Whenever something good happens, I still do that to this day.

I woke on the designated day, dressed in a sharp suit, and went to the John F. Kennedy Federal Building on Cambridge Street in Boston, adjacent to Boston City Hall. I went to the appropriate office and was asked to take a seat. Lisa was with me, and we were both excited. I had proved to the government of the USA that I was a worthy candidate for immigration, I was not looking to the government for assistance but rather was a taxpaying individual who did not take someone else's job. In actuality, I had created many jobs. I was a contributing partner to the US economy, having created three jobs in New York City and one in Cambridge. My one employee in Cambridge was Mehmet, a graduate student from Turkey. I paid all his fees for his master's program at Boston University and also gave him a salary. In return, he did whatever I asked of him in the business. I treated

Mehmet as a member of the family, including taking him out to dinner every night. We worked hard and had no time to cook. Mehmet was very cognizant of what I did for him, so he worked hard for me whenever he wasn't in school.

After waiting about 20 minutes, an INS agent asked me to follow him into a small, private office. The agent spoke extremely slowly when he introduced himself and asked, "Dooo youuu understand English?"

I said, "Yes, I speak it fluently."

Without smiling, he asked me what the three branches of the United States government were and to explain their functions. I explained the executive, legislative, and judicial branches, designed to have separate but equal powers to ensure and protect the rights of each and every citizen. It was also developed to put checks and balances in place to prevent a runaway government from committing acts of tyranny.

He then asked me who the mayor of Boston was. I answered, "Mayor Kevin White." Finally, he asked me how I got the money to start my own business since I was so young. As I was about to answer that complicated question, he smiled for the first time and said, "Independently wealthy?"

I answered, "Yes."

He then said, "Mr. Jesudian, I am approving your green card." He said I was free to go and could expect the green card in the mail over the next four to six weeks.

As he said this, I saw what looked like a green card in my open file, but I could not completely identify it from my vantage point. With a nervous smile, I said, "I am planning a trip to visit my family and was wondering if I could get the green card any sooner."

He asked me when I was leaving, and I said April 5, 1974. He thought for a brief moment and handed me the green card with my name on it from my file. I shook his hand, thanked him, and walked out of his office.

Chapter 14

GOD'S WORK IN A NUTSHELL

Talk about multiple mountaintop experiences! What had transpired over the past six years was monumental. I went to college, won a musical contest, made a boatload of money, was ridiculed by my friends and family, was grilled by a Consul General, traveled to New York City, started with a weak background in business, learned and created a successful business, lost it all to a shyster, moved to Boston, and started my very own business on a shoestring budget. As I slowly worked out of my bleak financial future, I became a legal immigrant resident of the USA. Phew! Even though I have a good dose of self-esteem and would love to take all the credit, under no circumstances could I ever tell myself or anyone else that I could have accomplished everything alone.

People who think there is no God are missing out on

so many amazing blessings. Some say, "If there is a God, why does he allow such hardship and evil?" First, there is a powerfully evil force that brings hardship and suffering upon humans, specifically to deter us from believing in God. Often, it seems that Satan is winning, but let's not forget, "It ain't over till the fat lady sings." The book of Revelation in the New Testament is the fat lady's song, so to speak.

Don't jump the gun. It will all end in God's timeline, not ours. Until then, all hardship, including death, is what God uses to grow us and give us character. It is the only way we can gain wisdom and help and guide another. They say death is the great equalizer, but I would add that struggle is also an equalizer. So struggle we must. There is definitely a God. He is a loving, caring, generous, and compassionate God. If you let him, he will bless you as he has blessed me abundantly. I give God all the glory. Amen!

Chapter 15

PREPARING TO LEAVE FOR INDIA

While I was in the process of getting my green card, I was not allowed to travel overseas. That was the rule in those days. As soon as I got it, I naturally wanted to visit my family in India because I hadn't seen them since I'd immigrated to the United States. I was also ready for a break after working 14-hour days for more than 750 days straight without a day off. But to make a trip to India, I needed to hire someone I could trust to run my store while I was away. Leslie Kaufmann had worked for me reliably and capably in the Lexington Avenue store in New York City when I was partners with Suresh, so I called her and set up a lunch meeting on my next trip to New York.

Leslie was an attractive blonde from Wisconsin who

had moved to NYC as an aspiring actress, as many young people in NYC did. These young thespians typically worked retail, waited tables, parked cars, or found any work with flexible hours so they could attend auditions and catch that big break. Sadly, most never got it, a reality that was always prevalent.

Leslie worked for me in the Upper East Side store in Manhattan. She was always smiling, up-beat, and engaging—fundamental traits to succeed in sales. She was also punctual and had a good work ethic. So when she had an audition, I would allow her time off. When I left NYC, Leslie stopped working for my partner and was waiting tables.

When we met for lunch, I asked her if she would like to take a break from NYC and come to Massachusetts for a few weeks to run the store for me. I offered to pay her $250 per week, a very good compensation considering a typical manager of a small specialty shop made $150–$175 per week in 1974. The minimum wage was $2 an hour, which translated to $80 a week as a starting salary for an unskilled worker, with a take-home salary of around $69 per week.

Here, I must take a moment to address the political rhetoric being dished out by the liberal left, progressives, and social Democrats. Minimum wage was never meant to be a living wage, nor will it ever be a living wage. In 1974, $2 an hour was not at all a living wage, and $10 an hour (which is a rough average of the minimum wage in all 50 US states today) is not a living wage in 2020, either. If we raise the minimum wage to $15 an hour, as some states have done, industries will raise prices within two quarters to accommodate the higher wage and cut workers' hours to keep costs and overhead down. Unemployment or underemployment will rise, and the new minimum wage will cease to be a living wage all over again within a matter of a few quarters due to increases in prices. Also, raising the minimum wage does a huge disservice to seniors across the board. They do not get enough of an increase in Social Security benefits but have to deal with the spike in costs of essentials and consumables.

People with zero skills in today's competitive world cannot expect the minimum wage to be a living wage. In order to expect a living wage, you must be willing to grow professionally or face an extremely difficult quality of life. Some people are born with talent. No one is born with skills. We acquire skills by humbling ourselves to learn and by applying our learning to grow in a particular field, whether the field is chosen or not. If we stagnate, we have only ourselves to blame. People who are 40 years old earning minimum wage are either unwilling to learn basic skills that will advance them to better wages or they have issues far bigger than the minimum wage can address. People who do the minimum will be paid the minimum. Those who are not willing to learn and move forward are their own worst enemy.

The government is not here to bolster people who do not want to learn. Remember, a democracy guarantees only two things: religious freedom and political freedom. Financial freedom is up to the citizens. The only people who should be well cared for in a democracy are citizens who are incapable of caring for themselves. No one should provide a living wage for citizens who refuse to learn, have a bad attitude, or are just starting out in life with zero experience. Even when you graduate from college, there is a starting wage, a minimum wage for a specific degree or position in a work environment. An individual with zero experience, fresh out of college, will start at a minimum wage for the position he or she is hired for. It is up to them to learn, grow, and move up the ladder of success. If they don't, they are destined to remain at that minimum starting wage. Therefore, if college graduates must begin their careers with a starting wage for a position and then improve themselves to progress upward, why shouldn't non-college graduates have to do the same? The lack of upward wage mobility is a totally self-inflicted circumstance.

But I digress.

Back to Leslie.

To sweeten the pot, I told Leslie she could stay in my fully furnished, one-bedroom apartment for free and use my new Mazda, gas expenses paid, as part of her remunerations. "It does not get any better," I said.

She was thrilled about working in Cambridge and living in Boston for a couple of weeks. It was a good change of pace from her NYC life—a win-win.

Then I gave her two nonnegotiable stipulations. I had recently hired Jack, an amazing salesman who was also a tall, athletic, good-looking fellow. Knowing Leslie to be a consummate thespian with an extremely healthy libido, I told her she must not date or fraternize with Jack. The second stipulation was that she could not allow anyone to drive my car. She rolled her eyes and said these stipulations were a given. She promised she would never do anything that would jeopardize our relationship.

I was thrilled that the store would be in good hands while I was away, and I had complete confidence in Leslie as a competent salesperson and a hard, dependable worker.

Chapter 16

THE TRIP TO INDIA

The exchange rate in India made each dollar in my pocket worth 10 times its buying power, and I had about five grand in cash. That is what upper-middle-class people in India made in a year. By Indian standards in 1973, I was loaded.

My parents lived in a city called Allahabad in the state of Utter Pradesh, India's largest state. Dad was stationed at COD (Central Ordinance Depot). When we arrived in New Delhi, my sister Cynthia came from Bombay to meet us at the airport. I was not the same man who left India three years prior. I had grown intellectually, emotionally, financially, and spiritually by leaps and bounds. I had been through some very heavy stuff, and I overcame it all. All my experiences had made me a much more confident individual.

Even my outlook had changed. When I left, I was a kid

just out of college dabbling in the music business. Now I was a successful businessman in New York City who had split from a crooked partner and struck out on my own in Boston, working my way up again. I had seen the good, the bad, and the ugly in a short time and had not only survived it but was thriving in spite of it all. To Cynthia, on the other hand, I was her baby brother, a wet-behind-the-ears 23-year-old. She assumed I got lucky, and everything fell into place for me. She didn't know what I'd been through, and, really, she didn't need to know any of it. As many do, she dismissed my success as being in the right place at the right time. But I didn't mind her dismissive attitude at all. I loved her unequivocally, was very close to her, and just accepted her as the first-born pulling rank over the last born. I was comfortable in my skin and not looking to prove myself to anyone, least of all my eldest sister. Though dismissive, she was curious about life in the United States, and I had to be sensitive to avoid sounding over the top or being misunderstood as a braggart. I deftly explained the great life I had in the USA while also emphasizing the grueling, hard work it takes to develop a good life.

After a superb lunch at the Oberoi Intercontinental Hotel in New Delhi where Lisa and I were staying, I told Cynthia I wanted to buy her something special. "What would you like?" I asked.

She looked excited but pulled the older sister routine with me. "You should conserve your money and not splurge," she said, not knowing I had the equivalent of 50,000 rupees in my pocket. She continued, "The amount you are wasting living in this posh hotel is itself too much."

"C'mon, Cynthia," I said. "I think I can swing it. What would you like?"

"Really?" she said. "Well, I would love a pair of really fancy high heels." Like many women, she never had enough shoes.

"Let's go to Janpath," I said, referring to a street with a plethora of stores, restaurants, and automobile dealerships. Janpath was in Connaught Place, the premier shopping area in all New Delhi at the time. She acquiesced, and the three of us hopped in a cab.

In Janpath, we shopped in a store known for high-end women's shoes. Cynthia looked at a sexy pair of stiletto strappy sandals made of dyed snakeskin. They were fuchsia and royal blue—just spectacular! Cynthia had good taste. She asked for a size 5½ and tried them on. She also happened to have pretty feet, nicely pedicured with what else but fuchsia toenail polish. The sandals looked spectacular on her, and she said they felt great. She was thrilled.

I was just about to say, "Let's get them" when she spotted the same pair in a black-and-tan version.

"Maybe I should be more pragmatic and buy the black-and-tan pair," she said. "It would go with more things," she mumbled.

Without waiting for a response, she asked the salesclerk for her size in the black-and-tan color. He brought the pair. She tried them on and looked absolutely fabulous in them as well. Now she was in the quandary women often find themselves in when they shop—which pair to get. She looked at the price and freaked. "I think I am going to think about it," she said.

I knew what that meant. I had dealt with women in my clothing stores for more than two years, and I knew exactly what she was doing. She was building a case in her mind against buying the shoes due to the price and other silly excuses.

Quietly, I told her I was buying her both pairs.

"No! I won't have it," she said.

"You have no say," I told her. "I am buying both pairs."

She then said, "If you do that, let me deal with the sales guy." When I asked what she was going to do, she said, "I am going to bargain, silly."

"This is a store, not some open-air bazaar without a storefront," I said. "They have a very high overhead and well-dressed, competent salespeople they have to pay reasonably well. It all costs real money." At her look of determination, I said, "Don't embarrass yourself. Let's get the two pairs of shoes, and we can all go back to the hotel and relax."

She would not have it. She asked the sales guy, "How much if I buy both pairs?" What the salesman said was priceless. With a broad smile, shaking his head like most Indians do when they talk, he said, "Madam, just buy one pair."

My sister was at a loss for words. I smiled and said to the sales guy, "We'll take the two pairs. Write up the sale."

I hoped my sister learned a lesson from that episode, but I was wrong. She didn't learn and never has learned life's amazing lessons throughout the years. I've learned through the years, time and time again, that you can be intellectually sound and ignorant at the same time. This is true for journalists, politicians, movie stars, athletes, scientists, doctors, engineers, lawyers, and many other so-called successful, intelligent professional people.

After the shopping spree, Lisa, Cynthia, and I traveled from New Delhi to Allahabad on a deluxe, air-conditioned, chair car express train. I loved getting on the train at 8:00 p.m. and waking up in time for breakfast the next morning as we rolled into Allahabad.

On the train ride, Cynthia and I spoke far into the night while Lisa slept off her jet lag. My sis told me how frustrated she was about working in India as a woman. It was a blatantly sexist society, more so in the 1960s than now. A man got promoted while a more capable woman was left behind. She said that often men made more money in lesser positions than women made in higher positions. I told her she should consider coming to the US and working with me.

She laughed and said, "How on earth is that going to happen?"

I said, "I can go back and see what I need to do to sponsor your immigration to the US." I told her about the US women's liberation movement led by former Playboy bunny Gloria Steinem (those in the know always knew that Betty Friedan was the real brains and guts behind the movement). "Living in the US beats living anywhere else on earth, anyway," I said.

She laughed some more and asked me how I would

pull it off. I told her I was the CEO of a budding business and would be able to swing it if she truly wanted to immigrate.

She said, "Of course I want to immigrate, but I cannot believe you can make that happen. I don't want you to play with my emotions."

I told her that if she would be patient, I would do it. I had never sponsored someone before, but I would get the required legal counsel and do whatever it took.

We reached Allahabad the following morning. Lisa soaked it all in, meeting members of my family, experiencing my exotic ex-country in all its hustle, bustle, colors, and smells—not to mention the variety of people in India blurring the cultural lines. She bought a bunch of exciting clothing and gifts for herself, her family, and her friends. India is truly a lot to take in on the first visit.

My middle sister, India (she was born in 1947, India's independence year, and was thus named after the country), who was married to an Air Force officer, came with her husband and their two boys all the way from Deolali, a munitions Air Force base south of Bombay. We all had the most exciting time.

Something very amazing happened during this visit that would change the entire dynamic of our family forever. Before I left for the US and as the youngest member of the family, I was hardly considered at all regarding anything that was happening in the family. Mom and Dad discussed family things privately and sometimes consulted with my two sisters, but never with me. I was just informed in passing. I didn't have a problem with that most of the time, but sometimes it got on my nerves just a wee bit. I was also acutely aware of being the runt of the litter and the drawbacks that came with it.

Since I had gone to the US and made good, started my own business, and had all this expendable cash, I was a young, successful Indian residing in the choicest of countries on earth, the United States of America. That changed things drastically. We went out to eat every night to the best restaurants, and I always picked up the tab. I bought my parents a new double-door refrigerator they had wanted for a while. Of course, they tried to talk me out of it.

I was like Daddy Warbucks for a few weeks, doing things for my family, especially Mom and Dad. Therefore, they now regarded my input. Even people outside my family paid close attention to whatever I said. At the officer's mess where I was once a punk kid, senior military officers were paying attention to what I had to say. On one occasion, my dad even asked me for advice. Once, my sisters asked our mother for advice, and she said, "Check with Leo. He can help you with that." I was blown away and quite enjoyed my newfound credibility. That shows that it does not matter how much someone loves you. You need to be successful to be considered credible and thereby given respect. You have to prove yourself to everyone all the time. I had earned everyone's respect after going to the USA and becoming successful according to their standards. Wow!

The vacation blew by, and soon it was time to head

home. And where was home? The US, of course. Remember, the first time I landed in New York, I felt I was home. Indeed, strange as it may seem, I never considered India home again after that cold day on January 13, 1971, when I landed at the John F. Kennedy Airport.

Chapter 17

BACK IN THE USA

When Lisa and I returned to Boston, we were truly happy to be home. But I was in for a rude shock. First, Leslie was having a roaring affair with Jack. Second, Jack had driven my car every day since I left and had had an accident with Leslie in the car. These were two very specific instructions I had left for Leslie not to do, and she had pledged she would not do them.

The car required extensive body work on the passenger side. Leslie apologized and said she would pay for the damage. I was miffed. "I thought I gave you two simple criteria to follow, and like a big shot, you said it was a given. Then you did an about-face and disregarded both of those things. And all you have to say is 'I'm sorry, and I will pay for the damage'? What about what I asked you to do?"

To top it off, they told me that business was slow. Well, it was obvious they were fooling around (in my apartment, no less) and not working much. I fired Jack on the spot and sent Leslie back to New York. I had never fired anyone before. It was not a good feeling, but in my book, broken rules have consequences. Whoever said that rules are meant to be broken must have had zero character. I made sure Leslie realized that I was not a cheap bastard. I did not want any money for the damage to my car. However, I was done with her, and she lost a good friend and ally.

Lisa was absolutely livid, and I had to calm her down while dealing with my own stress about the situation. The mess taught me an important leadership lesson. As a leader, not only did I have to keep my cool when crap hit the fan, but I was also responsible for counseling others to do the same. "This is obviously the cost of doing business," I told Lisa. I had chosen to be in business and was intent on becoming successful. So I had to learn and learn fast from my mistakes. If anything, I was a quick study, and I learned from both the good and the bad.

You know the saying: "When things happen, they happen in threes." Well, two things had already happened—Leslie had an affair and let Jack drive my car when she was specifically told not to. I became aware of the third thing a few days later. At the end of the month, when I was reconciling the bank statements, I was missing $1,500 in the business account. After adding all the receipts, rechecking the bank deposits, and balancing the books more than once, there was still $1,500 missing. I called Leslie and asked her about it. She said she knew nothing about it. Then she started to cry and said, "I cannot believe you are accusing me of stealing money." I had never mentioned her stealing anything. She chose to use those words. I realized that when people use words like that of their own accord, they are often guilty. Now it made sense when they said that business was very slow. It was slow, but not that slow. They had embezzled some cash receipts.

Now $1,500 was a good chunk of money in the early 1970s. For perspective, a year later, I moved into a fabulous penthouse in a brand-new building on Memorial Drive on the banks of the Charles River in Cambridge. It had two bedrooms, two full bathrooms, an oversized living room, a state-of-the-art kitchen, floor-to-ceiling windows, a spacious dining area, and a fabulous balcony with a spectacular view of the Boston skyline and the winding Charles River—all for a full market price of $550 a month. Stealing $1,500 was really a lot of money.

I asked Leslie if Jack had anything to do with the money not tallying, giving her an out. She kept crying and repeating how upset she was. Frustrated, I said goodbye and hung up. It was becoming extremely difficult to remain balanced after all that had transpired over the past two and a half years. I needed to continue trusting people and not assume that all people lie, cheat, steal, and disrespect others. However, sadly, most (not all) employees, no matter how capable or honorable they might seem, need very tight supervision or they cease to be capable and honorable. They often believe the boss makes too much money and that surely they deserve some of it, even if they have to take it. I dare say Leslie and Jack had a luxury vacation on me, and my trip to India cost me $1,500 more than I had anticipated plus the deductible on my car insurance policy.

Chapter 18

A FINANCIAL LANDSLIDE

The good thing was that it was spring, and business started to pick up. However, we had a long way to go. We got back into the swing of things, working hard all hours of the day all over again. Every Sunday, I set out for NYC at 5:00 a.m. and returned about midnight or after. All my suppliers opened their warehouses especially for me so I could buy goods, load them in my car, and return to restock the store. It was a grueling pace, but I had no choice. I needed and very much wanted to succeed and succeed big. God continued to play a huge role in my life by blessing me in ways that were downright outlandish.

I was in NYC one Sunday when Milton, a guy who supplied me Moroccan wedding shirts and dresses, asked me if I wanted the deal of the century. I was just getting out of the hole financially and could see light at the end of the tunnel. However, like most people on earth, I was eager to take the shortest route to the top.

He said, "Let's go to 34th and Lex. I want to show you something." Milton was my last stop. It was about 6:00 p.m. and still light out. Normally, I would head back to Boston about then, but I decided to check out what Milton had, needing to know what fired him up so much. I followed him into an apartment building where he opened a door and walked down a flight of stairs to a musty, dark, dingy basement. He turned on a light that was so dirty it was dim, and Milton grinned with his arms stretched out and his chin buried in his neck. "Look!" he said. "You like?"

After my eyes adjusted to the dark, I saw wooden blocks all dusty and filthy, stacked in rows of racking throughout the basement. "What the heck is this?" I asked him.

"Man, these are hand-carved, block printing pieces. They are from India, man—your part of the world. The hippies love them because they print their T-shirts, skirts, and blouses with this crap. This is as big as tie-dye, man. They sell for $12.95 each. I have 3,000 units I bought from this guy who was going out of business. I can let you have them for $3 each. Just nine grand in cash, and they are yours, man. You can get a quadruple markup and make a killing in your store."

He rattled all of that without seemingly taking a breath. I was amazed at how fired up he was. However, I was mad. I could have been on the Bruckner Expressway and far out of the city by now, yet here I was looking at nine grand worth of crap in a musty basement. I yelled at Milton for wasting my time.

"Woah! Relax, man!" he said. "I was just trying to help you out." I yelled some more, peppering my speech with all the horrible four-letter words I could muster and stomped out of there without a goodbye.

Back in my store a few days later, I was contemplating how to promote my business and increase my revenues. I was going to advertise in the *Real Paper* and the Boston *Phoenix*. I could not afford a radio ad, and TV ads were a fantasy at that time. Things were still slow. The weather in the spring in New England is a total crap-shoot. There could be one day in the upper 50s and 12 inches of snow the next day. While I was contriving various strategies, a customer walked in.

I struck up the usual conversation regarding everything other than the clothes on the racks, the jewelry in the showcases, and the accessories in the store. After the usual banter, she asked, "Whatever happened to the wonderful Indian hand block printing pieces that used to be available all over the place? I don't see them around anymore."

I was amazed. I had never seen or heard of those blocks, and now within a week, Milton had shown me 3,000 of them in a crummy basement in NYC, and a customer had actually inquired about them. I asked her why she was interested in them. She explained that she loosely belonged to an association that tie-dyed and hand block printed things for a hobby. I asked her how large her association was. She said, "About 500 people countrywide." Remember, it was 1974, and there was no Internet or e-mail. I asked her how she knew that many people with the same exciting hobby. She said she was a professor at Harvard University and that many of the members were in academia.

I asked her, "How many units would you be interested in buying for the group if, in fact, they were available?" I told her I had a guy in NYC who wants to sell a large lot, and I would need to buy the entire lot.

Her eyes lit up. "Well, we could probably buy about 1,500 units because no one can find them anymore."

"That is too bad," I said. "He has exactly twice that amount. I could not buy the whole lot and keep that kind of inventory on hand. It is not economically feasible."

"I think we would be able to swing it," she said. "Let me go back to my office and make a few phone calls and get back to you."

I asked her how much she would pay.

She said, "I used to buy them for $9.95 to $12.95 each. I can give you that."

"Ma'am, they are not available anywhere," I said. "This could be the last batch you will ever buy. It surely is worth a bit more."

"How much would they cost?" she asked.

"I think I can make a deal and sell them to you for $15 each."

"Deal," she said and firmly shook my hand.

"Why don't you write me a check for $1,000 as a deposit, and I will work on putting a hold on the stock and arrange for shipping while you go back and talk to

A FINANCIAL LANDSLIDE

your principal decision-makers. If it is a go, you can write me a check for a third up front and then the rest upon delivery. If there is no deal, you can come back, and I will return your check uncashed."

You must never let a deal slide if you can help it. Without hesitating, she pulled out her checkbook and wrote the store a check for $1,000. Remember this simple principle: Nothing happens if money does not change hands. I was excited as all heck. The last time I had a thousand-dollar day was on Lexington Avenue in NYC. Sure, I had to hold the check. However, she would never have written the check if she was uncertain about the deal.

As soon as she left, I called Milton. He said, "I never thought you would speak to me again."

"I was pissed," I said, "but I never hold a grudge. I am a businessman. I might have some good news. I think I have someone who might be interested in those crummy hand block printing wooden pieces you showed me on Sunday." I paused and then said, "The price you're asking is way too high, especially if you want me to take the whole lot." Then I shut up. Remember, I was a quick study. I had learned early in my sales career that after you say something important, you let it hang and say nothing. You let what you say sink in and have its effect. The next person to speak usually either spends money or loses money.

"I can't let you have them for less than $1.75 each," he responded.

"A dollar apiece cash in hundred-dollar bills, and we have a deal," I countered. Again, I shut up.

After a lengthy pause, he hissed, "You're brutal. How about $1.50?"

I said, "Milton, you're stuck, man. Take three grand in cash, and let's wrap this baby up."

"All right," he said, "you got it. Deal."

I was done. I was buying those hand block printing pieces for $3,000 and selling them for $45,000. Wow! I netted $41,500 because I had to cough up $500 for trucking. Now that is truly amazing. We're talking 1974 dollars. That was a huge windfall. Here's a little perspective on the value of the US dollar in 1974. A brand spanking new flagship Mercedes Benz 450 SEL with a steel electric sunroof, a Becker Mexico radio with cassette player, electric seats, electric windows, power rearview mirrors, electric antenna (remember those?), leather interior, and so on went for $15,438. You could buy a middle-class, single-family house with four bedrooms and two-and-a-half bathrooms on an acre of land in a very good Boston suburb for $30,000–$40,000. A US senator's salary in 1975 was $44,600.

This was a $41,500 profit on a deal that took 10 days to close, using the customer's down payment to buy the inventory. This made for a zero-dollar investment on my part. I ask every reader this: Does it get any better? Do things like this happen out of left field just by chance? I now ceased to be a believer; I was a knower. I knew beyond a shadow of a doubt that there is a God and that he was blessing me for my commitment and belief in him while honoring my hard work. This was monumental.

A FINANCIAL LANDSLIDE

My customer came back in a few hours and gave me $14,000 to make a full deposit of a third down. It was a done deal. I arranged for a truck to deliver the 3,000 hand block printing pieces from NYC to my customer's address in Cambridge. About a week later, I collected the balance of $30,000 upon delivery.

In a matter of 10 days, I went from struggling financially to totally coming out of the woods. I was on a roll. This gain also helped me a great deal in sponsoring my sister Cynthia. I had done all the paperwork, and I had my immigration lawyer in NYC work on her coming to the US. I sent her a PTA (pre-paid travel advice—airline jargon for a paid round trip ticket) and a formal letter of sponsorship. Then I filed the required financial statements with the US government through my lawyer to prove that should anything unforeseen happen to her, I would be 100 percent financially responsible, and she would never be a liability to the US government.

Remember, your word should always be true. It is very easy to forget your word when things are going well. I was a man of my word and never dropped the ball on my promise to my sister. I brought her to the USA and paid for all her documentation and legal fees to become a legal green card holder. Subsequently, she became a citizen. I was brought up with a solid regard for honoring my word. Things come into existence because someone honors his or her word. As stated earlier, we are made in God's image. As God spoke all creation into existence, we, too, can speak things into existence. Speaking things into existence does not mean speaking and doing nothing. It means following through with one's spoken word to truly honor one's word.

I intend always to honor my word, or I do not open my mouth. I honored my word with my sister and the promise I made to her on that train from New Delhi to Allahabad. I said I would bring her to America, and that is exactly what I did. I had to comply with the whole immigration process with all the documentation, laws, and finances to invite someone to visit the USA from a third-world country. If individuals came from Europe, Japan, Australia, or any other advanced nation, they could apply at the US Embassy for a multiple-entry tourist visa, buy a ticket, and arrive. I could moan and groan and think it is not fair. Who really cares about moaning and groaning? I did not have the time to do that. I had to accept my reality, move forward, and work with what I had or live a compromised life.

Illegal immigrants storming the border, sanctuary cities, catch and release, DACA (Deferred Action for Childhood Arrivals), and so forth are a calculated and planned degradation of America by the left. DACA is a very emotional issue. The left uses emotion to distort and achieve their goals. However, illegal behavior has disrupted families every day of every week of every year throughout history. Parents who make stupid decisions cause their children to suffer all the time. The Bible says that people's misdeeds will be paid for by their children and their children's children.

All children will deal with the consequences of their parents' decisions, both good and bad. When a parent commits a crime, the children face trauma and possible separation from that parent. When a parent goes into military service, the children are frequently uprooted or live long weeks and months without a parent, especially in wartime. My siblings and I grew up as army brats and were uprooted all the time. It was either comply or be separated. When a movie star, singer, or athlete has to travel to go on location or a tour, they are separated from their children.

Liberals pretend to care and then promote having children out of wedlock, guaranteeing a child is separated from a parent from birth. Liberals promote abortion as a woman's right to choose murder (the most heinous crime ever). Women definitely have a choice concerning what to do with their own bodies, as do men. However, when an egg is fertilized by a sperm, life has begun—a life free to make its own choices. The woman has no right to choose anything that would work against that separate, biological life with a separate independent heartbeat inside her for the next nine months. In fact, it is her duty and obligation to ensure the health and safety of that child.

Women try to blur the lines and call that separate life their body. Not so. A woman's right to choose is her right to choose whom she conceives the baby with. As soon as a child is conceived, the decision is set. Once you buckle in and the plane takes off, it is too late to abort your decision to fly. Abortion is infanticide no matter how one tries to spin it. A liberal friend told me she has control over her body. It is not the place of any person, organization, government, or entity to make a decision regarding her body. To that I agreed wholeheartedly. However, the second heart beating inside her is not her body, and she has zero rights over it for the very same reasons others have no rights over her body. She does not have rights over the other body growing inside of her. In fact, she is supposed to be the safest biological receptacle for the growth of that child to full term.

As was expected, she raised another emotional question: What about rape, incest, and the safety of the mother? I agreed that rape and incest are horrible, yet I said, "Why are you trying to justify aborting a human life, the ultimate form of control over another's body, while not wanting others to control your body? That is the definition of hypocrisy. We need one standard for all. We cannot have double standards just to suit our convenience." There are 55 million abortions worldwide every year, and that is absolutely heinous. It is genocide and nothing less. Liberals say we are to respect DACA because, through no fault of their own, the children were brought into a negative situation. With the exact same logic thrown back at her, I said, "Why then should we abort a child's life for no fault of its own? An unborn child is the most vulnerable life."

My liberal friend had no answer. I made my point.

Chapter 19

ALWAYS LOOKING TO GROW

It was April, and now with real money in my pocket, I sought to open a second retail store in Boston in addition to my store in Cambridge. I needed a second store for more than just expansion; I needed to create a job for my sister when she arrived. I found an awesome store in Copley Square at 545 Boylston Street at the corner of Clarendon with a huge For Rent sign. It was in the heart of Back Bay. I liked the location and decided to check it out. I was ready to expand. I called the number on the sign in the store window that read Hunneman Real Estate and made an appointment to see the space. Two sharp young executives, Jake and Joshua, showed up.

The space was gorgeous. It measured about 1,500 square feet, an ideal size for my kind of store. They wanted $2,000 a month and needed first and last month's rent and one month's security. I was responsible for the build-out, and I was told it was a triple-net New York lease. Being a New Yorker, I understood that term well. I loved the space and was excited about the prospects of having a second store—and one in Back Bay no less. We chatted about a few details and decided to meet the following Monday in Harvard Square. Jake and Joshua said they would bring the lease when we met.

On Monday, we met at the Wursthaus, a German restaurant in Harvard Square. After we ordered, they began. "We hope you are aware you will need to build out the HVAC (heating, ventilation, and air conditioning) as well."

I said I was aware and that there was no problem.

Then one of them said, "Did you know you are responsible for the build-out of the duct work for the HVAC from the roof?"

I told them, "Guys, I do not own the building. I know it is my responsibility to build out my store. I can do it for the store, but I am not going to spend money to enhance the entire building. You deliver the ductwork from the roof (13 floors high) to the store, and I will do the rest." As an aside, I asked them how much the ductwork from the roof to my store would cost. They said their general contractor could do it for $25,000. Adjusted for inflation in today's dollars, that was about $400,000 out of my pocket to invest and enhance their building—not my business. This meeting was over. They were taking me for a fool. The difference here was that they were MBA salesmen, and I was an entrepreneur. I could run circles around them all day long, and all they could do was look bewildered. I asked for the bill, pulled out a thick wad of hundreds, and paid cash for the meal. Before they knew what happened, I got up to leave. They were stunned and confused. I guess they had expected to start some sort of negotiations. I said, "You are looking for a sucker and not a businessman. I'm done." I walked out of the restaurant, leaving my uneaten meal while the two stupid executives were looking at each other totally confused.

Chapter 20

STORE NUMBER TWO ON THE CAPE

Around the beginning of May 1974, Lisa and I went to Cape Cod on a day trip. I had never been to the Cape but had heard so much about it. I was excited about exploring this famous vacation spot. Hyannis Port, Massachusetts, was the summer retreat of the entire Kennedy clan. We went there, had lunch in a cute little restaurant off Main Street, and took a drive. At the end of Main Street, we came to the West End. At the corner of Main and Sea Streets was a store for rent. In 1974, about 75 percent of the businesses in Hyannis Port were seasonal. Everyone was open for business from Memorial Day weekend through Labor Day weekend. Businesses had a 13-week season to make all the money for the entire year. In the 1970s, Hyannis Port turned into a ghost town after Labor Day. In fact, the whole village shut down. Without any experience with a seasonal retail business, I knew that all the stores should be rented, for Memorial Day was just around the corner. It was only a few weeks away, and business was going to boom. The stores needed to be stocked and ready to go, but one beautiful corner store was available.

I used the pay phone in the parking lot in front of Dunkin' Donuts to call the number on the For Rent sign. I spoke to Ben Finn who said he was on Main Street and that I should come to his office where he could pull out the file on the listing and give me all the details. In a few minutes, Lisa and I entered a storefront that housed Finn Realty. Ben was a burly, affable man with an engaging smile. Once we sat down, he told me what a choice location it was—a corner store with all glass windows on both Main Street and Sea Street. Two front windows flanked the door, which was in the center and set back about 10 feet. The windows were big, and the side panels were angled about 45 degrees to accommodate the entry door. Inside, the windows had a raised setting for displays such as mannequins.

I asked Ben, "If the store is such a good location, why is it still for rent so late in the season?"

He gave me a weak excuse about the deal falling through at the last minute with an out-of-town retailer. People talk in circles and make themselves look bad all the time. There should have been a waiting list to rent the store. I got down to the skinny and asked him how much.

"Not going to be cheap," he said. It was a 2,000-square-foot corner location in the best part of town. It had a room with a bath in the back that could double as a place to stay overnight in a pinch. He said it was $600 per month. "The landlord wants $2,400 up front, $2,400 on July 1, and $2,400 on August 31 at the end of the season." That meant I would pay the year's rent in three installments over the summer.

I told Ben I would rent the place for the first month's and last month's rent and would pay the rent on a monthly basis whether I was there or not. He said the landlord would not accept that.

I said, "If you don't even want to make a call, I am out of here," and I got up to leave.

Lisa was still sitting, and Ben said to me, "Wait! Sit down." He lifted the phone and called the landlord. He spoke very differently to the landlord. He said I was a successful New York businessman who had a store in Harvard Square in Cambridge, and then he explained my deal. "It would be great to rent the space." He listened, hung up, and then stood.

I thought there was no deal, so Lisa and I prepared to leave. Then he smiled and extended his hand. "Congratulations! You are the proud tenant of the store at 617 Main Street in Hyannis Port, Massachusetts. Now you can write me a check for $1,200."

I wrote the check, signed a standard lease, and collected two sets of keys in less than 45 minutes. Lisa and I drove to the store. It was perfect. There was beautiful, expensive, tightly-tufted, turf-green, wall-to-wall, wool carpet throughout the store. It had two dressing rooms and a nice room with a bathroom at the back of the store. All it needed were two 5-foot showcases, a middle desk with a cash register between the two showcases, racks, hangers, about $25,000 of merchandise, and a sign, and I would be in business. All the merchandise I needed was just a phone call away. I had excellent credit in the market and could get the store stocked for no up-front money.

Lisa and I could not stop talking about it on our way home. I went to NYC the following day and told all my suppliers I was opening a store the following week on Cape Cod. I ordered all the merchandise I needed and had it shipped. I also filled my car to the gills with goods and drove straight from NYC to Hyannis Port.

I arrived in Hyannis Port late at night with the car full of inventory. A few days later, my neighbor came running and said a UPS guy had 22 cartons of merchandise. He told me the cartons were stacked in my back room. Now I had all the goods I needed to open the store for the weekend. I just needed racks, hangers, and showcases. I hired a local sign company to paint my sign for $100.

I opened the store on Thursday and took in more than enough money to clear the check I had written to the landlord the past Sunday. In the 1970s, an out-of-town check took 10 days to clear. So in actuality, I opened the store in Hyannis Port with money I made in the store. I spent zero out-of-pocket dollars for another store. It was so much fun.

They say the rich get richer, and it's true. But people overlook why the rich get richer. They do so because they work incessantly and use their brains and experience to their advantage, preferably without hurting anyone. People who work a 40-hour workweek can definitely make a living and sometimes a good one. However, they almost certainly cannot become wealthy. Always remember that there are exceptions to every rule, no matter what. One cannot own a company and feel awkward about promoting the business anywhere and everywhere. The rich also become richer because they make the right decisions to build a successful enterprise. The rich become richer because just when things are comfortable, they get uncomfortable and take risks. The rich get richer because they pay all bills on time, even if it means taking nothing for themselves, to gain a credible rapport with vendors, utilities, the government, and employees. You cannot be a deadbeat and make it indefinitely. You must be a person of your word with banks, attorneys, accountants, employees, clients, customers, patients, passengers, guests, and any other person you have contact with. You must learn quickly from mistakes because there is no time to feel sorry for yourself. Be harsh with yourself, but forgive yourself immediately and move on. Then and only then do the rich get richer. The reason the store cost me no out-of-pocket dollars is that I did all the above and never failed to ask God for help.

On July 7, 1974, my sister Cynthia arrived in the USA on a tourist visa. I drove to New York's JFK Airport to pick her up. I told her I opened a store on Cape Cod and was going to teach her how to run it. She was excited and nervous because she had never worked in a store or sold a thing in her life. I asked her if she had seen me sell anything before I came to the US. She said no. I said, "Exactly." If I could do it, she could definitely do it as well.

She did very well, and we had a knock-out summer. By Labor Day, I had paid my rent every month, all my suppliers, all salaries, and utilities. I brought the invoices up-to-date, spent a reasonable amount of money, and still managed to save around $15,000 just from the store in Hyannis Port on Cape Cod. My store in Harvard Square had also done extremely well. Financially, I was in fairly good shape.

Chapter 21

STORE NUMBER THREE IN BACK BAY

Two weeks after Labor Day, I got a call from Peter Black, a real estate agent I knew fairly well. Peter knew I was interested in leasing a store in Boston. He said, "A Japanese restaurant is looking to close their takeout section and wants to lease the space to a small retailer."

I said I would take a look at the space. I went to Hai Hai, a nice Japanese restaurant, and looked at the storefront. The entrance was fabulous. It had two all-glass windows with a nice glass door set back in the middle, similar to my store on the Cape. The windows were built up about two and a half feet to accommodate displays. However, the store was a bit small, only 900 square feet. The location was superior to 545 Boylston Street, which was three blocks further down from the Boston Common (the store I had nixed a few months prior due to the numb-nut real estate execs looking to rip me off).

This store was located on the river side of Boylston Street between Arlington and Berkeley. It was the first block from the Common, and rent was only $1,000 per month. I made a deal to get the first three months rent free. After the attorneys drew up the lease, I took possession of the space on October 20, 1974, to build out the store. My actual first month's rent was due February 1, 1975. It was an excellent deal because I was going to clean up over Christmas and be cash rich to cover the cold, lean winter months when retail, for all intents and purposes, is extremely slow.

God was looking after me in a way that was amazing. It worked out extremely well, and I was on my way to having a very active retail business. However, February came with a new trial. It was an extremely cold day, and business was slow. I let my one saleswoman leave early since there was nothing much to do. (I never cut anyone's wages if I sent them home early.) I typically closed at 6:00 p.m., tallied the receipts for the day, and then proceeded to the Harvard Square store, which was open until 9:00 p.m. I sent the remaining salespeople home and was on the phone when I realized it was a little past 6:00 p.m. When I hung up and started to proceed to the door to close it, a guy came in. I was about to say I was closed when he asked me if I had a size 10 woman's shirt in pink. He said he needed a gift for his Old Lady. I smiled and said I did. I showed him a few shirts with several price points in pink, and he picked one. Then he hesitated and asked me if I had it in blue. I looked on the rack and found him a size 10 in blue. As I was about to turn around, he said, "Don't move, or I will blow your f'ing brains out." I felt what seemed like a barrel of a gun dead center on the back of my head. I froze! He then took the gun off the back of my head and told me to proceed to the cash register.

He was now in front of me, and I saw the gun aimed at me. It was not a good feeling at all looking at the barrel of a handgun in such close proximity. He told me to slowly open the cash drawer and hand him everything in it. I said, "Even the checks and charges?"

He said, "Shut the f* up, or I will blow your f'ing brains out! The cash!"

I handed him the cash gingerly—about $70—not much because business was slow, and the rest was in checks and charges. Then he told me to empty my pockets. Darn it! I had about $1,500 in my pocket. I gave him the cash. His eyes bugged out. In the 1970s, that was a ton of money, and people never carried that much cash.

His back was against the street, and he kept his gun aimed at my head. Right then, a woman came to the window and was looking at a dress on one of the two mannequins in the window. I said to him, "There is a woman, and she might come in."

"If she comes in, I will blow your f'ing brains out!"

A calm suddenly overcame me. I said, "Relax, man, you now have a lot to lose. Don't make a foolish move. Let me handle this."

"Shut the f* up, or I will blow your brains out!" The woman came closer to the door and was looking at the dress from the side. I never thought I would want so very much for a customer not to come into my store. I prayed that she would walk away. When she put her hand on the door, I was mortified. It seemed like a lifetime before she changed her mind, smiled at me, and walked away. I breathed a sigh of relief. The armed robber was smart enough to move so his body hid the gun, and she never knew he was holding me up.

He then ordered me to move to the back of the store. In the back room, he laid me face down on the cold, tile floor. I thought he was going to kill me. He hissed, "If you even try to make a move, I will blow your f'ing brains out, you hear me?"

I said yes, and he left. I heard the door shut and kept my ear to the floor as his steps receded. I then heard the front door open and shut. I waited for a few seconds and heard nothing. On my knees, I slowly opened the door where my line of vision was under the racks. I saw nothing. I walked out and locked the front door. I called Lisa and told her what had happened.

"Are you all right?" she asked.

"I am fine."

"Did you call the cops?"

"No, I called you."

"Call the cops!" she screamed.

So I did. I tried to reconcile the receipts for the day, but I could not focus. I was flustered and actually shaking with anger. I was angry at myself for not closing the store at 6:00 p.m. Then, I thought, I might have let the guy in anyway. I walked around nervously until the police arrived.

Two cops arrived in about 10 minutes. Boston's Unit 4 Police Station was a mere block and a half from me. They asked me if I was Leo and then butchered my last name. I said yes. They asked me for a description, and I told them the man was white, about five feet ten. He had not shaved in a week or so. He wore blue jeans and a worn-out black leather jacket and beat up black cowboy boots. He had not washed his hair and looked high on speed because he was very shifty-eyed and crazy looking. He repeatedly told me he would blow my f'ing brains out. They took down the report and said they would come the next day with a book of mug shots to see if I could identify the man.

The next day I called my insurance agent, Ray Goode. I said, "Ray, I was held up at gunpoint last night at the Boylston Street store."

"Are you all right?" Ray said.

I said I was fine and needed to see him right away.

"I am coming right over," he said. His office was in Chestnut Hill. About 45 minutes later, he arrived, and we talked a bit about the holdup. I told him I lost about $70 from the register and around $1,500 from my pocket. He advised me not to carry that sum of money around. Then I asked, "What do I need to do to make a claim?"

He hung his head and said, "Leo, I didn't cover you for armed robbery."

I was beside myself. I said, "Ray, I thought I

told you I wanted a very comprehensive insurance coverage. You said you knew exactly what to do, and we left it at that. How on earth could you cover a retail storefront in Boston without armed robbery and call it comprehensive?"

"Leo, I am so sorry," he said. "I will completely understand if you fire me."

"Everyone needs a second chance. I will give you just one more chance. Rewrite my policy, and get out of here. I don't want to see you until it's done."

Ironically, about two-and-a-half years later, I got held up again. This time I was amazed at how calm I was. I had done this before. I went through the entire routine all the way up to calling Ray again. He came and asked me how much I had lost. I said about a hundred in store cash and another $1,100 cash out of pocket. He had another hangdog expression.

"What now?" I asked.

"You have a $1,000 deductible."

I burst into laughter. "You insurance guys are bastards." I fired Ray Goode on the spot.

I now had three retail stores and was moving on up. Because I needed to haul inventory from New York to Boston every week, I needed a reliable automobile. I traded in my Mazda RX3 rotary engine station wagon for a full-sized Ford Country Squire LTD station wagon with all the bells and whistles. I also started paying my key suppliers at the time of purchase in cash with $100 bills to get a 20 percent discount. It was all legitimately invoiced. My margins had increased as I had decreased the cost of my goods from 50 percent to 40 percent and didn't drop the selling price. So instead of having a keystone markup of 100 percent, I now had a markup of 150 percent. At the end of the year, that would cover a ton of overhead and increase the profit margin, and my stores remained a competitive option for any woman looking for attractive clothing. I was quickly becoming savvy in business and cutting my teeth at negotiating with suppliers and manufacturers.

Chapter 22

PARENTS' MAIDEN VISIT TO THE USA

In March 1975, about a month after I got held up, I visited India and asked my parents if they would like to visit the USA. Their eyes lit up. My credibility in their eyes was now flying high. I had successfully given my oldest sister a job, sponsored her, paid all her expenses, and given her an awesome opportunity to live and partake in the American dream. My mother looked down and said, "Son, you should save your money. You just took Cynthia to the USA last year, and that was very expensive. Though we are flattered and would really love to visit, I really don't think it is a good idea right now. Moreover, your dad will have to get cleared by the Ministry of Defense to travel abroad. I am told it is quite a task."

That last sentence indicated that my parents had already inquired about what it would take for them to take a trip to the USA. I looked at them and said, "Let me let you in on something very important about me that you don't seem to know. I am brutally honest with myself, and I will always protect the goose that lays the golden eggs, with God's help. That is to say, I will do nothing to jeopardize my business because I am aware that it is more than just a business. It is something God has given me, and I need to be a just steward of it, especially since it does so much and will do so much more for the family. Mom, if it was going to be a problem, I would never have brought it up. I am of the opinion that if everyone does what they need to do, I can swing it. Mom, I would love nothing better than to show you the country your father studied in and inspired me to go to."

Both my dad and mom said almost in unison, "What do you mean, 'if everyone does what they need to'?"

"If you and Dad take care of your end," I said, "and get the required clearance from the Ministry of Defense, I will take care of all the necessary things that need to be done on my end. I want you both to use all the clout you have to get the clearance taken care of efficiently."

They got very excited. I looked at Dad and said, "How long would it take for you to get the Ministry of Defense clearance?"

"Sixty days or so," he said.

"Start the ball rolling right away," I said, "and also get passports. You can visit the USA from the middle of June through the middle of August. The weather is ideal in New England and New York during those months."

I returned to the US and called my lawyer in New York. He said it would be a piece of cake to get them a tourist visa since my dad was still working as an active government employee in India, my mother was deeply rooted in India, they were older, and their son was in the USA. We got all the details taken care of without any challenges. I sent them two PTAs on Pan Am and waited for them to get government clearance.

They arrived in the United States on June 10, 1975. It was their very first trip abroad. It was oh so exciting! I took them everywhere in my new Ford Country Squire, and the summer was a blast. They saw Cape Cod, New York City, Washington, DC, and everywhere in between. My dad loved the rest areas with the Nutmeg Inns and Howard Johnsons, which were prevalent in the 1970s along I-95 in New England. We stopped routinely to use the facilities, have coffee and snacks, and fill up with gas.

Dad found the highways and the infrastructure in the USA to be absolutely superior to anything he had ever seen. Even though my middle sister was still in India with her husband and two sons, the rest of us had a fabulous family time all summer long. Cynthia was dating a nice Jewish boy nine years younger than she was and married him the following year. (She is still happily married to Steve, and now their son Mark is 40 years old.) The six of us—Mom, Dad, Cynthia, Steve, Lisa, and I—ate dinner every night together in restaurants or at home unless Mom, Dad, and I were gallivanting somewhere out of town on business. They had a grand old time checking things out and experiencing America the Beautiful.

It was a really good time, but I never skipped a beat professionally. When we took a trip, it was for business. Mom and Dad came with me, and we all had a blast. I kept working all hours of the day. Every night, I asked Mom and Dad if they wanted to ride with me the next day or stay home and relax. Invariably, they wanted to ride with me. They wanted to see it all, have a great time, and spend time with their son. I took them with me everywhere. Business was good, and life was great. I am amazed that life stops for people who have family visiting. I incorporated my family into all I did.

The summer did cost a good bit of money, but in essence, it was what I was working so hard for. I approached everything with the ultimate goal of life satisfaction. Too much of society has been brainwashed into chasing job satisfaction. It is highly productive for the people in power to promote that philosophy because they need workers at every level to focus on their jobs. It makes employees feel as if they wanted it all along and that nothing was ever forced on them.

If and when average people finally realize they never wanted job satisfaction to begin with, it is too late; they are embedded. When individuals feel they have no place to go, then comes self-talk and justification. Think about it. The world needs workers in order for the elite to live the lives they want to live. Thus the heavy brainwash. Schools, colleges, and universities are designed to fulfill that worker need. Education has become the conveyor

PARENTS' MAIDEN VISIT TO THE USA

belt for workers at all levels. From CEOs who do not own the company to the maintenance worker and cleaning crew, it is common knowledge that the world cannot function without workers.

But when these people want to do their own thing, they need to know the rules of the game. If you want to be in business and live the dream, the credo to live by should change from job satisfaction to life satisfaction. For me, life always trumped work. Hence, without even knowing it and thinking it through, I was all about life satisfaction. How many times have you heard people in the arts say things like this: "Find your passion, and chase it so work is never work." That only works 1 percent of the time. The other 99 percent of the time, people who chase their passions are usually broke. I say, chase what gives you a great life, and indulge in your passion on your own time.

There is another statistic we need to be aware of. A Gallup poll states that two-thirds of all people in the workforce are dissatisfied. What does that mean? They have subjugated themselves to working in a job they do not like, and that job pays them just enough to keep them there. You see, employers are extremely savvy. The people who chase job satisfaction live compromised lives. There are only a fortunate few who have both job satisfaction and life satisfaction. They are successful athletes, actors, singers, writers, and the like. The cold, bare facts are that the majority of people work for a living and focus on job satisfaction. That becomes their self-talk mantra, if you will, and they neglect the true quality of life. In fact, many tell themselves they love their jobs when in actuality they don't even like them. It is apparent. Look around, and you will see it everywhere. If you have to do whatever it takes to pay the bills and survive, why not focus on life satisfaction? By the way, anything other than living the dream is just surviving—just plain existing.

A very small minority (and I am part of that small minority) chases life satisfaction. We know to do whatever it takes, to work very hard with a specific life goal in mind. I have never cared about job satisfaction. Due to that single difference in philosophy, people like me with integrity, a sense of honor, and a good work ethic finally live a dream life. Is it easy? Absolutely not. It is harder than anything, especially when starting out. However, finally you get to live your *dreams*!

Now we must put "do whatever it takes" into perspective. I recommend having standards. For example, unethical and illegal acts do not justify life-satisfaction goals. For example, it is not right to deal in narcotics and do whatever it takes to live the dream. Also, engaging in prostitution to put oneself through law school is a bogus justification of illicit behavior. Many have worked hard legitimately and put themselves through school. Prostitution is a horrible quality of life, no matter how temporary it might be, and it rarely is. The behavior leaves scars for life, and scars do not bode well for life satisfaction, not to mention it is very much against God's principles.

Let's face it. No one should live to work. We all should work to live. As a matter of rule, what you achieve should outweigh what you must do to achieve it. In other words, the goal should supersede the effort. That logic implies that life is way more important than work. It was a given with my philosophy and upbringing that the effort should be legal and ethical.

It was a momentous year in 1975 both in a business and personal sense. I was realizing many of my dreams with focus, hard work, zero complaining, and persistence in the things that proved worthy of my effort. When you do what needs to be done to achieve a goal, the effort is worthy. I kept learning from decisions that were both right and wrong and kept moving forward. The takeaway was to keep doing what is right and what works toward the end goal and eliminate everything that does not work, not only from my physical being but also from my mental space. Easier said than done, right? I don't know who made up the phrase "easier said than done." Isn't everything easier said than done? That statement comes from a person who does not intend to do anything.

Another simple rule is this: Never excuse yourself to yourself or others. Equally as important is this: If you don't excuse yourself, then you should not excuse others either, especially family and friends. That is not to say you should be confrontational or unforgiving. It means you should not buy into sob stories or get sucked into a mode of sympathy for everyone's excuses. Always save sympathy for serious mishaps, but maintain wisdom. Always remember, we all have our own customized crosses to bear. No matter what we say to appease a situation, we must know the situation in our hearts and minds, and act accordingly.

HARD WORK AND THE AMERICAN DREAM

My mentor, Dexter Yager, wrote a wonderful book called *Everything I Know at the Top I Learned at the Bottom*. That's a profoundly amazing title for an extraordinary book. Never disallow someone at the bottom to experience the bottom thoroughly—they won't learn what they need to if they don't. People frown at the bottom, but it is the bottom that teaches us what we cannot learn otherwise and builds character. It hardly matters if one is born at the bottom, in the middle, or at the top. All that matters is that we learn at the bottom and get out of it.

People born at the top also have to hit bottom if they want to be relevant. If anyone thinks the elite minority has it good 365 days a year for their entire lives they need their head checked. If you are languishing at the bottom for too long or indefinitely, it is because of your personal behavior and nothing more. You can definitely hit bottom due to forces outside your control or due to personal mistakes. However, staying at the bottom is self-inflicted. Instead of learning through mistakes and moving up, many want to languish in their misery and have the government take from the top and give to the bottom—a handout. That, ladies and gentlemen, is not America.

Politicians are opportunists. They capitalize on everything they can capitalize on. They promise to take from the top to give to the bottom. In every society, there are people who live for handouts and vote for these liars. Shame on people who live for handouts. Only those who absolutely cannot fend for themselves need to be taken care of by the government. America was built on dignity, and there is no dignity in living for handouts. I am all for a safety net to help someone with a hand up when things go awry. However, the abuse of a hand up is what gets to me. We need to work for everything we have, and if we don't work for it, we do not deserve it. In fact, by choice we should have less. The only exception to this rule is an inheritance.

The new world is teaching that we should all have everything all the time, even if we do not deserve it. Humans are by nature takers. If they are given everything all the time, they will cease to be creative, enterprising, and productive. They will do pretty much nothing. Giving things to people for nothing does not make a good society; on the contrary, it destroys a good society from the core.

Since being astute and savvy with money is being conservative, what is being liberal? Is it burning through money, living above your means, being debt-ridden, and wanting the government to bail you out? Well, then, I would rather be conservative. I am human as well. When I was young, I dreamed of getting things for nothing at least now and then. However, at an early age I realized what getting something for nothing does to the human spirit. Since then, I have never wanted something for nothing.

I was a solo flyer and a successful one at that. I started to read biographies and histories, and I noticed a common thread. A lot of them mentioned mentors. I personally thought mentors were for people who needed help and could not achieve on their own. To some extent, that could be true. Some of us can do it on our own and really don't need anyone but God. Well, a good mentor is appointed by God to guide you in your earthly decision-making process and keep you on the straight and narrow. I completely overlooked that truth for many years.

High-level athletes, actors, singers, and dancers all have coaches and mentors at the peak of their game. Why is it that mediocre people think they don't need a coach or mentor while the rich and famous do? The problem is that a mentor does not pursue a protégé; the protégé must pursue the mentor. I wish I'd had a mentor to guide and coach me when I was a young man. Learning from your mistakes works great, but it is more efficient to learn from someone else's mistakes. You must be humble enough to learn from someone else. If you find yourself constantly questioning your mentor, you are not ready for one. It is a fool who wants to learn everything from their own mistakes.

Here, I must clarify the word *simple*. Many confuse it with the word *easy*. The English language needs to be understood and understood well. English is my third language. My first language is my mother tongue, Tamil (a root language like Latin and Sanskrit), spoken in the south of India. My second language is Hindi, the national language spoken in India. I categorically reject the flimsy excuses about not understanding the subtleties of the English language. Live by your word; don't excuse yourself or another. Laziness contributes to failure. So let's get back to the word *simple*. To differentiate one word from another similar word, we must seek the opposite of both words. If the opposite coincides, they mean the same. On the other hand, if the opposites do not coincide, they have different meanings.

The opposite of simple is complex, and the opposite of easy is hard. The words *simple* and *complex* have to do with understanding, while the words *easy* and *hard* have to do with effort. Therefore, simple and easy are two different words that must not be confused with one another. Something very simple to understand can be rather hard to accomplish.

Allow me to give you a sports example. Basketball is a very simple game to comprehend. There are very few real, enforceable rules. I can explain the rules of the game in less than 15 minutes, and the person to whom I explain it will be able to follow and enjoy watching the game. However, doing it is hard. Why? All you have to do is bounce the ball while moving forward. Do not take more than two steps without bouncing the ball, stay within the confines of the court, and release the ball from possession before the clock winds down to zero. If you are tall enough, you can actually stuff the ball into the opposing basket and score two points. If you foul within the semi-circle (the arc), the opposing team gets two free throws, which, if done right, gets them two points. You cannot goal tend or attack an opposing player if it has anything to do with anything but the ball. Last, you cannot go out of bounds and hold possession. I think that pretty much covers it.

So why is such a simple game to understand so hard to play? It is because there are five players anywhere from six feet five to seven feet tall specifically there to obstruct you from accomplishing your goal. It is foolhardy to think that something simple to understand can be easy to do. It's mandatory to become extremely adept at bouncing the ball, feigning a run down the middle only to twirl 360 degrees and pass the ball to an open teammate. Life has more than five six-foot-five players trying to hinder you from scoring. If you buckle, life will be all over you, and you will lose the game and even the season.

Here is another example. There are only seven notes in a C major scale with five sharps or flats thrown in for various effects. In those few notes exist all the songs written from the beginning of time and in every genre. That's very simple to understand. With that fairly simple concept, try writing music, playing it, and creating melodies, harmonies, and lyrics people like. It is extremely hard to do. In fact, it is so hard to do that people who do so successfully are supremely wealthy because they are paid for their rare ability and talent.

In January 1976, I was in India when Cynthia called from the US. She was so excited. She had been summoned by INS (now ICE) for an interview for her green card. She was going for the interview in a few days and was beside herself. I was ecstatic and equally excited since we had waited more than 18 months for this to happen. She went to her interview, aced it, and got her green card. Cynthia is six years older than I. She never liked working for her kid brother. She just did not like the role reversal and was not happy. Her ego could not deal with having to work for her youngest sibling.

PARENTS' MAIDEN VISIT TO THE USA

As soon as she got her green card, she called me. After the initial congratulations and the chatter with our parents, she told me privately that she was leaving for Switzerland to be with her boyfriend, Steve, who was going to hotel school in Glion. That was the first time she had said she wanted to quit working for me. I was not surprised since I knew she would do so. What I failed to see was that she did not care for me at all. She had bought a ticket and was leaving that evening. I said, "Cynthia, I am coming back in four days. Please wait until I get there. We need to celebrate this wonderful event—getting your green card and all that."

She refused me point blank. I could not believe my very own sister would leave my business in the hands of untrained people for four days after everything I had done for her. I tried to talk to her, but she grew belligerent. I hung up, feeling grieved. She not only did not care for me, she did not care for anyone, because at this point, the business was the goose that laid the golden egg for the entire family. She couldn't wait five days for me to return from an international trip? Nope, she up and left for Switzerland to be with Steve, abandoning the very job that delivered to her an amazing life.

The good thing is that Cynthia and Steve have now been married 42 years and have a 40-year-old son, Mark. Cynthia was the scholastically brilliant one of us three siblings. However, she always had a lousy attitude, and her only claim to fame is that she raised a son. I don't mean to be rude, but even ants have progeny. She was smart enough to have done anything she wanted to, but she didn't do anything with her life because she considered everything an aggravation. I do not relate to that at all. You see, life is interesting and not always what we want it to be. I love Cynthia, Steve, and Mark. However, I do not relate to that kind of behavior at all. It's not a recipe for success.

My corporate lawyer, Gordon Martin of Martin, Morse, Wylie & Kaplan, called me one morning to say he wanted me in his office the following Monday at 8:00 a.m. I reminded him that he worked for me and that I was the one who told him when I wanted to see him. I said, "Gordon, you have it all backwards."

"Leo," he said, "the reason I want you to come to my office on Monday at 8:00 a.m. is to meet the next President of the United States of America."

I chuckled at his attempt to be a salesman. "Well, Gordon, who might that be?"

"None other than his excellency, the former governor of Georgia, Jimmy Carter."

"Who?" I asked.

"Jimmy Carter!"

I laughed out loud. "Gordon, are you part of his campaign?"

He replied with an emphatic yes.

I said, "Gordon, I am a green card holder, not a citizen yet. I am not a good candidate for your meeting since I cannot vote."

Gordon replied without missing a beat, "I don't want your vote; I want your money."

I had to hand it to him. He was good. I told him I would be there, and he said, "Bring your checkbook."

I went to his office at 8:00 a.m. on Monday. When I entered 31 Milk Street, I saw Gordon Martin in the lobby, nervously pacing the floor and biting his nails like a young, insecure boy.

"Get hold of yourself, Gordon," I said. "Stop biting your nails like a nervous little schoolboy." He snapped his hand, spit the little nail out of his mouth, and smiled nervously. "You're not seriously thinking that this guy Jimmy Carter is going to win, are you?"

"Jimmy Carter is going to be the next President of the United States of America," he answered with conviction in his eyes. "Let's go outside to the sidewalk."

I said, "Let's go upstairs to your conference room and act dignified."

He walked out, ignoring me, and I followed him. He was excited, talking a mile a minute about the future and what Jimmy Carter would do for the United States. I was amazed at how animated this seasoned, successful Boston lawyer was. Then he said in a high-pitched voice, "There they come!"

I leaned out toward the street and looked for a black Lincoln Continental stretch limousine. When I didn't see one, I said, "Where?"

He pointed and said, "There."

There was a five-year-old or so silver-blue, full-sized Ford LTD station wagon with a darker dull blue driver's door and Georgia plates. Gordon Martin was waving his hands, and it pulled curbside. A heavy-set, dark-haired man got out of the driver's door, looking beat. He stuck out his hand and introduced himself as Bert Lance. He went on to become Carter's Office of Management and Budget Director. Carter got out of the passenger seat, also looking beat. They had been driving all night. I thought they would take an early morning flight. They were on a shoestring budget with no real funds. I was mortified and felt sorry for them.

We went up to the conference room. I expected Gordon's select clients to be in the room, standing room only. Come to find out, we were the only ones scheduled to be there. I had a one-on-one with Jimmy Carter and Bert Lance. Carter was genuinely a fabulous, God-fearing and intelligent man. He spoke of his mother, Lillian Carter, being a health volunteer in India in 1966. I was impressed with his knowledge base and the fact that he was an ex-Navy nuclear submarine officer and also a devout Christian. I wrote Jimmy Carter his first campaign donation in New England for $250.

I was amazed later when Gordon Martin was right. Jimmy Carter won the Democratic nomination and then became the 39th President of the United States of America from 1976 to 1980. He proved beyond a shadow of a doubt that it took way more than being a good, intelligent person to run the most powerful nation on earth. He was a micro manager with zero vision, making him the second-most inept president America has ever known. However, anybody anywhere who truly knew him knew he was truly a wonderful human being.

Chapter 23

STORE NUMBER FOUR IN NEWPORT, RHODE ISLAND

It was early 1977, and Jimmy Carter was president. It was just after the bicentennial year. America had celebrated its 200th anniversary as a republic, and the entire nation was still in an exuberant mood. Newport, Rhode Island, was home to the America's Cup, the trophy awarded to the winner of the oldest and most prestigious yacht race in the world. There was a buzz about the America's Cup race in September 1977. Australia was the big contender. (America eventually won the race for 132 years, consecutively fielding 24 challenges from 1879 to 1983. They finally lost to Australia II in 1983, and the cup moved to Australia for the first time ever.) Newport was always a festive, upscale place in the summer and peaked during the America's Cup race when it was held. The race is on whenever a qualified yacht club challenges the club holding the cup. When New York won in 1851, it took England 20 years to challenge New York to a rematch.

One Sunday morning, Lisa and I decided to go to Newport for brunch and feel the joy of visiting the lovely coastal town that was home to the Vanderbilts and other extremely wealthy families. There was also a buzz about the upcoming America's Cup race that September. We had a great time. After brunch, we decided to walk around and check out the shopping area and the yachts on the waterfront. While there, we saw a good location at a brand-new development called Brick Market Place adjacent to the waterfront, the very waterfront where all the yachts come to dock. I called the real estate agent, and before I knew it, we were off to the races to rent another store. Within six weeks (again just before Memorial Day), I had opened a new store. The clientele was over-the-top wealthy, and we did extremely well. Though it was still a seasonal business that lasted a little past Labor Day, the money was great, and it was another successful store.

Chapter 24

FIRST FORAY INTO IMPORTING FROM MEXICO

At this point, with four stores, I was buying goods from various designers, manufacturers, and importers. This experience made me consider importing my very own goods. That way, I could buy and land goods in the US for much less than I was currently paying for them at a high overhead New York showroom. This method would enable me to wholesale a major portion of the shipment and get a higher markup on the retail in my four stores. I put the numbers on paper and did my due diligence. It was a go.

Later that year, I traveled to Mexico to buy sweaters, wedding dresses, and wedding shirts. The first experience in Mexico was hilarious. I had been buying woolen Mexican sweaters from an importer in New York for about two years. Those sweaters were used on the TV show *Starsky & Hutch* and were very popular in the fall months. I decided to take my first trip to Mexico to source them directly. I bought a round-trip ticket without a clue about where to go, what to do, or even what to expect.

I landed in Mexico City after a fairly tiring flight. I freshened up and went down to the lobby of the Sheraton Hotel and asked the concierge where I could find the classic woolen sweaters that were so popular. He said, "Señor, they are everywhere." I left the lobby and took a walk down the road. Part of becoming successful is entering into uncharted territory, even though you are nervous, and acting as if everything is old hat. Most people will not do so and therefore do not gain the advantage that adventure offers.

Like the concierge said, the sweaters were in stores everywhere. I had paid the importer in NYC $15 per sweater, buying 100 at a time and selling maybe 250 per season. They were available for $9 per sweater in Mexican retail stores. I was excited about that. I walked into a store and asked the owner of the establishment what it would cost if I bought them wholesale. He said $6 each. "What if I buy 500 units?" I asked.

He thought for a moment and said, "$6.50 each."

I laughed. "That is funny," I said. Then I thought that maybe there was a language problem. So I repeated that I wanted to buy 500 units. He looked incredulous, rolled his eyes, shrugged his shoulders, and said, "I know, I know."

FIRST FORAY INTO IMPORTING FROM MEXICO

I looked equally incredulously at him. "If I buy 500, you increase the price?"

He said, "Señor, I have to work harder, no siesta, not see family much. I charge you more for the sacrifice I make."

I was blown away by this lazy, unenterprising logic. There is a reason that Mexico is not a financially strong nation while sitting south of the most economically successful nation on earth. It has nothing to do with the people and their abilities but everything to do with a general work ethic. They would rather sit around and shoot the breeze than haul butt and make a killing. Everyone who hauled it in Mexico was making a killing. But the bulk of the population was hanging out and not doing much. I bid the store owner good day and left.

I asked everyone I bumped into, including the wait staff at the restaurants, where these popular sweaters were made. When I discovered that there were wholesalers and manufacturers in Guadalajara, I traveled there the next morning and shopped all day until I finally found a company with a volume of goods and reasonably sharp individuals heading up the enterprise. I purchased 500 units for $3.75 each, which amounted to a landed price of approximately $5 in Boston after duty, airfreight, and brokerage fees. I wholesaled them for $13, undercutting the New York market price, and retailed them for $29. I reordered the sweaters twice, making my total buy for the season 1,500 units. I upped my volume to 300 sweaters at retail because, being flush with stock, I never lost a sale. Another little nugget: Never knock inventory.

Retail brought a gross profit of $24 each or $7,200. I sold the remaining 1,200 sweaters at $13 for a gross profit of $8 each, or $9,600. The total gross profit on the sweaters amounted to $16,800. I invested the money on my usual cash outlay with the importer in NYC but made almost 400 percent more with the sale of just one item in 1977 dollars. That is good business.

Of course, I worked harder and took a leap of faith in myself and trusted God, as usual, to do the rest. I cut out the middleman, got off my duff, embraced the unknown, and risked a $1,000 round-trip visit to Mexico to learn that Mexico was lucrative. I was growing in revenues, experience, and global business. On 250 sweaters from the wholesaler in NYC, I invested $3,750 and made a gross profit of $3,750 per season—100 percent markup. Now, with a cash outlay of $7,500 ($5 x 1,500 sweaters = $7,500), I had a gross profit of $16,800, which increased our profit margin to 107 percent and gross revenues by 224 percent. This was not rocket science, not even mathematics. It was simple arithmetic, along with a basic willingness to get a little uncomfortable, travel to unknown lands, have a work ethic to source goods, and have a sole purpose of doing commerce. The takeaway is this: Not only did I raise our revenues a lot, I increased the profit margin as well. With this simple attitude and clear thinking, I not only had four retail stores but also a budding import company that allowed me to start a small wholesale business as well.

I worked 14 hours a day, seven days a week. Though I was young, energetic, and exhilarated by the winning,

FIRST FORAY INTO IMPORTING FROM MEXICO

my workload was downright grueling. Everyone I knew was having parties on the weekends, going away on vacations, watching sports, and attending barbeques, but I was constantly working. My vacation was going on a business trip, fighting jet lag, and working all day in a faraway land. There is a very serious reason why the majority of immigrants who come to America for a better quality of life are more successful than the people who are born and raised in the USA, the ones who have a jump start but don't take advantage of it. People like me don't back off because we did not immigrate to the US to be mediocre; we came to excel. I tell people in my seminars, "I didn't immigrate to the USA for the weather, the food, or to be middle-class. I immigrated to the United States to become an American, excel, and make a killing." I was not going to settle for anything short of that.

Chapter 25

IMPORTING FROM AFGHANISTAN

With my success in Mexico, I decided to source unique (the key word is *unique*) products that fit the image I wanted to create in my retail stores. I had a vision of providing every woman who walked into my stores with a high-quality, fashionable wardrobe from all over the world, one that enhanced her image as both sexy and classy. I also began to lightly manufacture my own brand of women's clothing under the name Eclipse.

I bought Afghan sheepskin coats from a guy named Mohammed in NYC. One day Mohammed told me he wanted to move back to Afghanistan, his homeland. I told him I was confused. "Why would you want to do that?" I asked. "You are living in NYC, an amazing place, and building a nice business in the coveted US. You have a great future."

He told me that his wife and children were back in Afghanistan and that they spoke Pashto and no English. It would be hard for them to adapt to life in the USA. He also said he had amassed a reasonable amount of money back home, which was not hard to do since the US dollar went much farther in Afghanistan than it did in India (and boy, did it go far in India). He asked me if I would take over his business in the US and import the goods from him. That way, he would be able to go back and focus on the procurement and production of goods. "If you agree," he said, "you would assume all the business I have developed in NYC."

At this point, I was not going to overthink things. It was a prudent move on his part and a good deal for me. He had come and developed a market and then decided to return home to service the market he created. He had accomplished what he set out to do—to get a foothold in America. He was looking for an honest, upright person to take over the operations in the US, and that person was me. I told him I would definitely be interested in importing from Afghanistan. I was already selling his products. I later realized that I was one of his biggest buyers. We made a deal, and I was set to import goods from Afghanistan.

In early 1978, I flew to Afghanistan and found interesting products I could market in the US. However, the best product I spotted was an Afghan wedding shirt. It was a round-necked, long-sleeved, simple pullover shirt. It had two cloth-covered buttons on each side of the neck, and when the buttons were undone, it had a slit that went almost to the shoulder, enabling it to easily slip over a person's head when the buttons were open. The shirt could be worn tucked or untucked. It was cut straight at the bottom (no shirttail), with two four-inch slits on either side.

So, what was so exciting about this simple shirt pattern? The front of the shirt was hand-embroidered from the neck all the way to the waist in a square, apron-style front, similar to a tuxedo shirt with pleats on an apron front, except the Afghan wedding shirt had a wider front and no collar. When buttoned, it had a round neck. It was made of a medium-weight, soft rayon. The embroidery was silk yarn in the same color as the fabric. This technique made the tuxedo bib pop and glisten while the rest of the shirt was a flat color. So the effect was a simple silhouette with a spectacular shimmering bib on the front of the shirt in a rectangle from the round neck all the way down to the waist. It was subtle and yet spectacular at the very same time. I got this shirt in black on black, white on white, red on red, navy on navy, fuchsia on fuchsia, and so on. It was simply a very elegant shirt.

I paid $3.50 FOB (freight on board) in Afghanistan, and after freight, duty, brokerage, and handling, the shirts landed in-house in Boston for roughly $5.25 each. I also made my own variation of the shirt but with the sleeves having tight gathers on the shoulder and a tightly gathered cuff. The cuff was a bit wider than usual, with double buttons and loops to match the ones on the neck. The sleeves looked like a pirate's shirt sleeves. I had the cuffs over-stitched in a close diamond pattern to give it some extra zing like the embroidered bib of the shirt. That cost me 25¢ more, so the landed cost for me after duty, freight, and brokerage fees was around $5.50. The men's and women's wedding shirts were exquisite. I had mid-calf-length matching skirts with the same embroidery on the bottom six inches of the skirts and drawstring pants with the same embroidery at the bottom four inches of the pants. They were all the rage. I became known for them. I wholesaled thousands and retailed hundreds a year. I went to Mexico for sweaters, wedding dresses, and hand-embroidered peasant blouses. I bought exquisite hand-embroidered Romanian peasant blouses for $25 each (that was exorbitant in those days for a blouse) from Bucharest; they retailed between $125 and $200 each. I gradually developed a great cross-section clientele, which included some celebrities. I even saw my clothes worn by people featured in some very popular magazines. That helped business immensely.

In Guatemala, I manufactured fully-lined women's blazers made of boiled wool. They were trimmed with gorgeous woven, textured silk ribbon around the neck and a notched collar to the bottom and all the way around the back of the hem. I had the cuffs trimmed as well, all the way to the elbow. The ribbon crawled up the forearm in swirls, ending in a point that pointed toward the shoulder. The same was done around and from the back shoulder to the center back of the neck. The ribbon

IMPORTING FROM AFGHANISTAN

was stitched in swirls going downward and ending in a point a third of the way down the back. The jackets were red, black, or white with color-on-color ribbon. For variation, I contrasted the white and red blazers with black ribbonwork and the black blazers with white ribbon. That gave my customers a variety of six blazers to choose from or buy more of.

The contrasting ribbon blazers were downright dramatic and very popular with musicians and people interested in making a splash or a fashion statement. I landed the blazers in the US for $20 each and sold them for $80 retail. I did not wholesale the blazers because they were an exclusive item in my stores. My cost was 25 percent of the retail price, a very good margin. I sold 200 units from September 1 through Christmas in my two nonseasonal stores. I never had to mark them down. Without really knowing it, I was building an excellent brand. Even though I had majored in physics, chemistry, and mathematics in college, I was making one helluva living on artistic endeavors I never went to school for, first in music and now in fashion and design.

Afghanistan was also working out very well for me. I took four trips a year and bought a lot of goods that I both wholesaled and retailed successfully.

On one of my trips to NYC, Jonathan, a friend and business associate in NYC who manufactured a sportswear line, said he wanted me to take a look at something. We went from his showroom on 1411 Broadway to the garage. I said, "I thought you wanted to show me something." As I spoke, the elevator opened, and one of the attendants drove a gleaming Mercedes 450 SEL out of the elevator. I looked at the car and said, "That's a beauty!"

"That's my new car," Jonathan said. "That is what I wanted to show you." He asked me to go to his house on Todd Hill (an exclusive area of Staten Island) and have dinner with him and his wife, Ellen. He said, "We can come back to the city in the morning around 10:00 a.m."

So I left my year-old fancy Peugeot 604 (the latest four-door iteration of Peugeot's competition to the Mercedes Benz E series and BMW 5 series cars) and hopped into the new, gleaming, silver 450 SEL. It did not drive; it glided quietly with great power and amazing aplomb in and out of lanes, leaving most of the traffic behind. The front seats, sunroof, rear seats, rearview mirrors, and antenna were all powered. The cabin was so well-sealed and sound-proofed that when I closed my door, my ears popped. All of a sudden, my fabulous Peugeot 604 wasn't that appealing to me anymore. It was late 1978, and my 1977 Peugeot 604 that cost $11,900 was a hands-down loser to Jonathan's 1978 450 SEL that cost $26,300. It was not a fair comparison, but I was smitten. A few months later, I sold my Peugeot 604 and bought a brand spanking new Mercedes Benz 450 SEL in a metallic brown with a tobacco, all-leather interior and all the bells and whistles I could possibly have. Boy, was I realizing a boatload of dreams! And to think, I was only 27 years old and just getting started.

In 1978, I moved from my beautiful penthouse apartment on Memorial Drive in Cambridge overlooking the

Charles River to an even more beautiful, brand new, never-lived-in penthouse apartment in 4 Longfellow Place with a doorman and a view that literally took people's breath away when they entered. I would send for my parents every summer after my Dad retired in early 1977. The protocol was that I would send them tickets in April for them to come in late May and stay through July. It was great having them visit and experience America on a regular basis. The fire chief palmist was right; my mother was traveling a lot internationally. Since I worked all the time, I took them everywhere with me—to New York, Cape Cod, Newport, and anywhere else. They enjoyed exploring the shops and restaurants while I did my business. Life was good even though I was working long hours. I simply told myself that this was what I needed to do because I was an immigrant. But I was acutely aware of one critical fact: I lacked time, the most important commodity in life. We are all a summation of our self-talk. I kept telling myself that my children and my children's children would reap the rewards I was creating, and though I yearned to relax and enjoy myself, all I did was work more.

Chapter 26

DIVERSIFYING MORE

In the summer of 1978, something very interesting happened. I was in New York having dinner with a few friends in a very popular Indian restaurant called Rasoi, which had received rave reviews. The reviews were well-deserved for the food was awesome, the ambiance very cool, and the service great. The prices were high because it was on 57th Street between 5th and Madison Avenue in NYC and also because it had received high reviews. High prices never bothered me, even when I was struggling in life and broke. If the price of something was high and I wanted it, I just worked harder to have the money to buy it. I never complained about paying higher prices for things I wanted. The choice was entirely mine. I could either work hard to have it or do without—a fairly simple approach to life.

Here I must take time to address something critically

important. Today, there is a lot of rhetoric about income inequality. People who work hard are portrayed as somehow hindering the individuals who either don't work, do the minimum for minimum wages, or work a regular 40-hour workweek and have a middle-class life. I am all about taking care of anyone who for a physical or mental reason cannot earn a living. I am also all about a finite, time-sensitive safety net for hardships that people find themselves in and that are out of their control. However, income inequality has always existed since time immemorial. It exists today and will exist always, no matter what anyone says or does. God gives us all free will to do as we wish and bear the consequences of our decisions thereafter. I categorically reject the notion that individuals can make a decision to do the minimum amount of work or do the average amount of work and demand a superior life. I also think it is counterproductive for people to be disgruntled and jealous of people who strive for and accomplish a dream.

It is even more counterproductive for people to be jealous of heirs of fortunes derived from parents who chased a dream. From the beginning of time, handing down assets to progeny has been expected. It is not something new. The very same people who are upset about others inheriting their parents' assets will leave their children an inheritance if they have it to leave. This jealous hypocrisy should stop.

Way too many people think a 40-hour workweek is going to make them wealthy. A 40-hour workweek is designed to make workers work efficiently and make a decent living at best. In all my years of business, traveling internationally to all parts of the world and interacting with thousands of people, I have never met a successful millionaire who works a paltry 40 hours a week. The sentiment of jealous, lazy people is this: Let's make a lot of noise to get something for nothing. Leaders throughout the ages have promised the masses more and then give them just enough to retain power. How has their behavior helped the poor? People have been played like a fiddle by their leaders. The upper classes have worked their tails off, used their God-given minds to their fullest abilities, made mistakes (as we all do), never given up or felt sorry for themselves, and made out. The masses keep going back to vote for the lying leaders like a moth to a flame or more realistically a battered person who keeps going back to the batterer.

The heirs of fortunes also have choices. They can increase their wealth with hard, smart work, or they can squander it away. We can criticize their choices, but we do not have a right to deprive them of their inheritance. Here is the irony: When heirs squander their wealth, people consider them worthless, spoiled bums who came into a lot of money and blew it. When heirs increase their wealth into bigger fortunes, they are deemed greedy and privileged. Jealousy knows no bounds.

But when you're demanding someone else's wealth, you are the one that happens to be the greedy one. The Bible calls this greed covetousness. There are three forms of wanting what you do not have—envy, jealousy, and covetousness, listed in ascending order of wantonness.

Covetousness is the highest form of undeserved want. God has specifically commanded (not asked or suggested) us to not covet. Yet politicians use this base human emotion of covetousness to their political advantage. They promise to take from the rich (taxation is a modern way to usurp from the wealthy) and give the general public free this and free that, thus preying on human covetousness. Politicians know full well that they will deliver little or sometimes none of their promises yet with the much higher taxation garner more power and opulence for themselves.

In medieval times, people who did nothing were the poor, and some resorted to illicit behavior by becoming thieves. In modern times, a lot of them vote for politicians on the left who falsely promise them handouts. Then there are the cunning who game the safety net created for the real needy and steal. The so-called progressive politicians penalize those who are successful and hardworking and promise to reward the lazy. In all nations, the truly wealthy are less than 1 percent of the population. The majority are not rich. It is a very cunning prudence by politicians to get the popular vote. These so-called bad, wealthy people who work hard are the ones who create jobs and make up the most important part of a winning economy. Also remember that these wealthy people make up the very economy that categorically funds the government.

Politicians always say the wealthy need to pay their fair share. Does anyone care to know what exactly fair share is? A truly fair share would mathematically mean the exact same percentage rate for all. Anything else means the people who make more are subsidizing the people who make less. Grammatically and mathematically speaking, a graded taxation is not fair at all. Am I against a graded taxation? Actually, yes. However, I can live with it. What I abhor is the false narrative that the rich need to pay their fair share when the rich pay higher taxes and are the ones who create jobs and hence even pay more taxes. When government says it creates jobs, I do not agree on pure logic. Successful enterprises create jobs and feed the economy that creates taxes that allow the government to have jobs, and thus it comes right back to wealthy, successful people—the engine that creates it all. I encourage journalists, citizens, and professionals to call out every politician who corrupts the English language by distorting the meaning of words to suit their 100 percent false narrative.

Even the banking system has caught on; it operates on the premise that people want what they cannot afford. They have devised an advantageous methodology called the credit card. It is a fact that everyone wants to relieve the other of their money. It is called commerce. The difference is that the government forces us to give up our money through taxes, and private enterprise entices us through advertising and marketing. I prefer private enterprise's process since we have the right to choose rather than the government's process that forces citizens to surrender 25–50 percent and more of their income. Government also has the worst track record for the stewardship of public funds. Government is important, or there would be anarchy. However, minimum government, please! Government should only do what private enterprise cannot.

Here is where government can play a good role. It should step in and not allow usury rates to be charged to people for credit. People are encouraged to lease cars they cannot afford, buy houses they can hardly put a down payment on, wear clothes bought with credit cards, make minimum payments, and rack up interest rates anywhere from 18–23 percent. So when you see that woman with a real Louis Vuitton bag, don't be surprised if she has no health insurance, doesn't pay her college loans, and votes for progressive (communist) candidates for local, state, and national offices. Why? She wants free stuff. If you see that guy driving a leased BMW, don't be shocked if he is delinquent on his tuition loan payments, has no health insurance, and has the ability to credit card a round of shots for patrons he does not even know at the local pub. Oftentimes, these false big shots pretend to be for the environment—green this and green that— but burn a crapload of high-test gas in their BMWs and SUVs instead of bicycling their way to work according to their vocal positions on the environment. They all vote Democrat!

I was a Democrat for years and always found myself voting for conservative candidates. I decided to take a look at why it was so. I found out I am fiscally conservative and socially tolerant. God says it is not for us to judge, and though that is hard to do, I have trained myself to comply. Being a businessman, I have learned to evaluate and not judge. Some would say, "Is it not the same?" I say, "Absolutely not." To evaluate is to do due diligence. I try my darnedest not to judge. However, if someone asks me, I am forthright with my opinions, regardless of whether or not my opinion is popular or politically correct. Most people who are politically correct are downright liars. They pretend to care and understand when actually they are placating others to look good in the public eye.

Back to the restaurant in NYC. I called our waiter over and asked if the owner was there. He politely told me that the owner was there and that he would tell him to stop by our table. I thanked him. The owner was a savvy, sharp-looking Indian man in his late 30s. He sauntered over to our table and said, "You asked to see me, Sir?" I introduced my friends and myself and said, "I have something to ask you."

He affably said, "Go ahead."

I told him I loved the food, atmosphere, and service. I told him I was from Boston and came to New York City every week on business.

"What business are you in?" he asked.

"The clothing business," I said. "I have a showroom on 1411 Broadway." I asked him if he would ever consider opening a restaurant in Boston. It is a very cosmopolitan city with a quarter of a million students of higher learning from all over the world. A fine Indian restaurant such as his would do fabulously. I further told him that there was only one Indian restaurant in Cambridge, Massachusetts, owned by a couple. The man was an MIT (Massachusetts Institute of Technology) engineer, and his wife cooked. The food was downright bad, yet they were busy every day of the week because they were the only game in town for Indian food.

He laughed and said, "Why would I ever want to go to Boston? It is such a hokey town. There is no way I would consider that."

"I am in Boston and have a good business reputation. I can get you a lucrative long-term lease and a liquor license in a prime location. I would do all of that for no financial gain. I would just like a nice place to eat some good Indian food and take family and friends to a reputable Indian restaurant. All you would have to do is bring your expertise, and it would be a hit."

He nodded his head and flatly said, "No way. Not Boston."

Now let' see how God works and the opportunities he creates.

Back in Boston a few months later, Hai Hai, the Japanese restaurant whose owner was my landlord, decided not to renew its lease. I had to either get another place or hope the new tenant who leased the premises would allow me to continue with my sublease. I had met the two owners of the building when I signed the sublease from Hai Hai, and I had built a nice relationship with one of them. One of the owners was a Harvard professor named Marshall Goldman, and his partner, Manny (Emanuel) Joseph, owned a successful book-binding business. The restaurant was in a four-story building on Boylston Street where only the street level was rented to Hai Hai and me. The three upper floors were vacant, and

DIVERSIFYING MORE

I would concur that the restaurant used it as storage—a very poor use of choice office space in the heart of the city. There was a small elevator that could transport four adults.

Suddenly from nowhere, God put a thought in my head. Why not sign a lease and open up that Indian restaurant I wanted the owner of Rasoi to open? My mind started to race. I had a good friend named Leo Romero who owned an extremely successful Mexican restaurant in Back Bay that I frequented often. It was called Casa Romero. I asked Leo to have dinner with me so I could pick his brain. He said for a free meal of his choice, he would not even inquire about the subject of the conversation. So we got together for dinner at the fancy Café Budapest at the Colonnade Hotel off Copley Square. Over dinner I told him about my plan. I asked him about the pitfalls I could expect when I opened the restaurant. I never asked him whether I should open a restaurant. He unequivocally told me I should never open a restaurant since I was not a cook or a chef. He said it was a foolhardy thing for me to embark upon. He said I had no justifiable reason to go into the restaurant business. I kept trying to ask him about the pitfalls, and he kept telling me that I was crazy and that there was no reason to further discuss the matter. He also made certain I knew I would thank him for his sound advice once I had thought things through. Though the food was awesome and cost an arm and a leg, the dinner was a bust from a business perspective.

One of the key qualities of a winner is to be stubborn

about success and invest in your capabilities, discipline, and ability to learn and apply the knowledge you gain through experience. I decided not to heed Leo Romero's wrongful, unsolicited advice. If someone else could do it, why couldn't I? Restaurants had been around for eons, since cavemen. When the hunters brought back the meat they hunted, they sold or bartered it for services from the rest of the clan. Then someone cooked it and served it to the community. That was their form of a restaurant.

    I met with Manny Joseph, who was elated to rent me the building. He said he would talk to Marshall Goldman who would surely like to see me flourish. I had gained a reputation for getting things done and being a moneymaker. In a week, my lawyer had a lease in hand for review, and we were on our way. I told Kenny Soble, my attorney, that I needed a full liquor license for my restaurant. He said it would be expensive—$1,500 a year. However, the city of Boston had stopped issuing liquor licenses, and I would have to purchase an existing license that someone else was selling. I would have to pay the current market value and legally transfer it, which would cost me legal fees over and above the market price of the license. Licenses were issued to locations. The owner of the license was named on the license as the manager of record in those days. There would be hearings with the ABC (Alcohol and Beverage Commission) for the transfer approval. The whole process could cost between $30,000 and $35,000.

    Here is something for all to comprehend: Government rules and regulations inflate costs. Bureaucrats create this inflation, whether they know it or not. Another example is a hackney license. However, today, Uber and Lyft have upended that whole game. Instead of letting the market handle the demand, government wants to get involved in everything since licenses are really an added tax that winds up inflating the cost of goods and services.

My attorney told me that Dinty Moore's restaurant was going out of business and their liquor license was for sale. They wanted $27,000 for it, and it would cost about $33,000 with filing fees, yearly dues, and legal expenses to go through the ABC hearings for the transfer to my location. I gave him the green light to get everything started right away.

In January 1979, I flew to India to look for chefs. I also wanted to get authentic Indian furniture and décor that was exotic yet hip to make this restaurant the talk of the town. I looked at beautiful hand-carved chairs and expensive silk brocade for upholstering the cushions. I also shopped for authentic Tandoor ovens (horsehair plaster barbeque ovens for those authentic Indian Tandoori meats and breads). I went to the foremost preeminent restaurant for Mughlai cuisine, par excellence, called Moti Mahal in Old Delhi. The food at Moti Mahal was so delicious that no words could do it justice. Every morsel was a cornucopia of tastes. I asked my waiter if I could speak to the chef. He bowed and said, "Certainly, Sir." The chef—Vijay Sharma—a soft-spoken, rotund man with a captivating smile, showed up at my table. After speaking to him in Hindi for a few minutes, I asked him if he would like to come to the USA and work for me in my new restaurant I was opening in May 1979. His eyes lit up, but he said nothing. I asked him if he could meet me the following day, and he nodded.

"Meet me at the Oberoi Intercontinental Hotel in Nizam-ud-Din west in New Delhi," I said. "Here is my card. Does 3:00 p.m. sound good?" He nodded again, and I said, "See you tomorrow, then," and I shook his hand.

The word *Mughlai* comes from the word *Moghul*, and the cuisine is the food prepared for the Moghul emperors. The chef from Moti Mahal (*Moti* means "pearl," and *Mahal* is "palace") was the preeminent chef in all India, specializing in authentic Mughlai cuisine. I was wary about Vijay Sharma showing up at 3:00 p.m. the next day. He looked excited but clammed up suddenly when I mentioned his coming to the US. He never really answered me; he just nodded his head. But he surprised me and showed up on time. I told him I would send him an official job offer and invitation once I got back to the US. I would take care of all the legal and financial requirements, and he should get a passport ASAP so it would not delay the process. I also told him I would pay him $400 (30,000 rupees) per week. He almost fell off the chair. He would have been ecstatic with $400 a month. I also said I would make a nice room with a full bath above the restaurant that he could stay in for free. That meant he would live for free, eat for free, earn more than he could imagine, have all his legal bills taken care of, and immigrate to the first world. He was so delighted that he wanted to touch my feet (a sign of utmost respect), but I stopped him from doing so. I had hired my chef. Hooray!

DIVERSIFYING MORE

I think I was more ecstatic than he was. However, I knew I had to do much more before I returned to Boston. I told my parents I was going to Bombay. If something happened to Vijay Sharma, I was dead in the water because I could not cook. I needed insurance, so I was going in search of another chef in Bombay who did not know Vijay. While in Bombay, I lived in the Taj Hotel, and I loved the food there.

I bought silk brocade fabric in two colorways for the cushions, one in the upstairs dining room and one in the downstairs. One colorway was blood red, silver, green, purple, and a hint of yellow and pink. The other colorway was royal blue, silver, green, purple, and a hint of yellow and pink. After ordering 150 hand-carved chairs in a place called Darya Ganj in New Delhi, I left for Bombay and checked into the famous Taj Mahal Hotel. Vijay had an amazing style that made his food stand totally apart from any I had ever tasted. His food was delicious with intricate sauces, gravies, and marinades. Each morsel was a blend of flavors never encountered before, dancing on your palate. Every dish was distinct in ways I never knew dishes could differ. The first night I was in the Taj, I saw a guy in a chef's hat in the main dining room where I was eating dinner. In a five-star hotel, there are many chefs. I asked the guy who the executive chef was. He said, "I am, Sir. My name is Javed Ali."

I smiled. "Javed, when you have a moment, please come to my table. I would like to talk to you."

He said he would do so. In about 10 minutes, he came and asked if I liked my meal. When I told him it was

HARD WORK AND THE AMERICAN DREAM

delicious, as usual, he asked, "Have you been here before, Sir?"

"Every time I am in Bombay, I stay at the Taj," I said. "Can I ask you something?"

He shook his head from side to side as most Indians do and said, "Please, Sir, go ahead."

"Where have you been trained?" I asked. "You cook so well."

"Sir, I have trained with the best and have also been abroad in Europe. I worked for five-star hotels in Germany and Switzerland before I got the executive chef's position at the Taj."

"Great!" I said. "Have you ever been to the US?"

He shook his head again from side to side and with a sort of sad look said, "No, Sir. It is a dream I have not accomplished as of yet."

I was excited. I asked him if he was serious about the dream to live and work in the US. Without hesitating, he said, "Sir, everyone I know would do anything to live and work in the US."

"I don't care about everyone," I said. "I am asking you, Javed."

Almost before I finished my sentence, he said, "But of course, I would love that."

I lowered my voice and said, "I am opening a restaurant in May this year. Do you have a passport?"

He nodded yes.

"I will give you $400 a week and a nice room with a bath. Are you married?" I said.

"Sir, my wife and children will remain in India." He

had just agreed to work for me by saying his wife and children would remain in India.

"Javed, can you meet me at the café at the Sun-n-Sand Hotel on Juhu Beach tomorrow at 3:00 p.m.? I want to talk to you separately." He said yes, and I gave him my business card and shook his hand. I was flying high. Two for two—not bad. Not just any two, but the best-of-the-best two.

I finished my meal and went up to my room. I suddenly worried about something I had not thought of. Vijay Sharma was a Hindu, and Javed Ali was a Muslim. Even if they seem to get along outwardly, Hindus and Muslims have a deeply divisive issue since the partition (India and Pakistan) in 1947. Also, who would be the boss? There could be only one head chef. Yikes! I was rethinking the whole strategy. Finally, I realized I was unnecessarily getting into a tizzy. So I let it go and concluded that if push came to shove, I would take Vijay Sharma and get a lesser chef to work under him. If it was God's will, all would be well.

As usual, I was early and got a table overlooking the swimming pool. Past the pool was the Arabian Sea. It was a nice, a hot day, about 95 degrees Fahrenheit, and the pool was full of frolicking men, women, and children. The restaurant was quiet and cool. Bollywood music drifted softly over the sound system. I ordered a cup of filtered coffee (commonly known in India as a pour-over cup) and settled in. At 3:00 p.m. sharp, Javed met me at the restaurant. We made some small talk and got right to the point. Immediately I expressed what I thought would be a challenge. I told Javed I wanted two chefs and three assistant cooks since the restaurant sat 135 people in two dining rooms, another 35 people in the bar area, and, when the weather permitted, an extra 35 people on a sidewalk café. "I hired a man named Vijay Sharma who is the head chef at the Moti Mahal in old Delhi," I said.

I was blown away when Javed Ali told me he knew all about Moti Mahal and Vijay Sharma. Then he said something that stunned me. He said it would be his honor to work under Ustad (the guru of chefs) Vijay Sharma. Wow! The executive chef from Taj Bombay was willing to humble himself to that degree. I realized this Vijay Sharma guy was very highly respected by his peers in the industry. He was a real superstar! I gave both Javed and Vijay $400 a week, living quarters, free food, and a three-week paid vacation. I even covered the cost of their flights to and from India once a year. And don't forget, they got to live and work in the USA, and I paid all their legal expenses to get them a green card. Wow! I was thrilled beyond compare. A win-win for all.

From their perspective, they never dreamed they could earn that amount, and furthermore, they were never treated with such consideration and respect. What's more, they'd both dreamed of living and working in the USA. The takeaway here is that when you chase your dreams, you often help others realize their dreams as well. It must be noted that in 1979, the maximum these two amazing chefs could earn in India was about 4,000 rupees ($400) a month, and they had to pay all their own living expenses. I would cover it all and pay them $1,732 a month (remember, there are 4.33 workweeks in a month, except for February). Converted to Indian rupees, that would translate to 17,320 rupees per month. That would allow each of them to send more than double what they earned home and have enough money to reasonably enjoy life in the USA. They were ecstatic!

While I was in India, I bought two Tandoors in Old Delhi in a place called Kashmiri Gate for 600 rupees ($60) each and shipped them by sea (surface), which was an extra $350. However, the two Tandoors cost me $15,000 to install in my restaurant.

Here's why.

The Fire Chief at the Boston Fire Department had never seen a horsehair plaster, open-hearth oven before and considered them a fire hazard. The Chief was completely taken up with it. He wanted me to build a fireproof structure on the base and all around it. I had to hire an architect to draw the plans. Then I had to schedule a hearing to have it approved. The hearing again involved Attorney Kenny Soble and his exorbitant legal bill. The plans needed to be amended a few times with specific language for the specific fire-retardant tiles, fire-retardant materials used in the cement, fire-retardant bricks, and special lining in the interior walls of the structure that housed the ovens. For each additional plan, there was a fee for the architect and an additional hearing with lawyers' fees. Finally, when they approved the build, I was one of a half a dozen restaurants at that time in the US that had a genuine working Tandoor. I can safely say that I had the first fire-department-approved pair of Tandoors in all New England in 1979. After all was said and done, we had a soft opening for the restaurant on Sunday May 13, 1979 (there's that number 13 again). Peaches & Herb were singing their number-one hit song, "Reunited" (got to get a little music trivia in here), and God was good, and life was exhilarating.

A second thing happened in 1979. My accountant, Sy Goldberg, called and said, "I have the most amazing news for you. I just finished the financial statement you asked for. After doing the balance sheet for your business and the profit and loss statement, you, Sir, are a millionaire."

I smiled and thanked him for the good news. I was working so hard and with such focus that it never even occurred to me that I was becoming a millionaire. All I was doing was trying to create a quality of life for myself and my loved ones. He seemed genuinely surprised on the phone, which I felt was a little rude. I said, "Sy, you seem surprised."

He said, "Leo, you did it in such a short time—and made it seem so easy."

I laughed and said, "All professionals make what they do well seem easy." I then got serious and asked him how I had made it seem easy.

He said, "In a matter of six years, you did what most people who make it to millionaire status take a lifetime to accomplish."

Remember, this was 1979. No Internet, no social media, and no cell phones to do things wherever you were. In short, it was a very low-tech world for business.

I said, "Sy, first of all, it was not easy at all. I worked

when everyone else was playing, sleeping, or just plain being lazy and watching mindless TV and sports. I focused on working almost all hours of a day, building a foundation for a great life in the greatest country in the world. I also didn't take the routine two-week vacations most people take or enjoy weekends like most people do. Instead, Sy, I chose to do what others don't so I will have what others won't. It took me 15 years, not six years, to become a millionaire. Keep in mind, I had to keenly use my mind and whatever experience I learned every single day to achieve success. I was not privileged, but I strived to create a privileged life."

"How does 1973 to 1979 make 15 years?" he asked.

To this silly, one-dimensional accountant I said, "Last time I checked, Sy, the workweek is 40 hours, right? I have worked 100 hours a week. That is two and a half times the normal week. Multiply six years by two and a half, and you get 15 years of concentrated hard and smart work using all my God-given faculties. You see, Sy, I could not lose. I certainly did not immigrate to the USA for the weather or the food. I came to thrive, excel, and contribute, not to be a mediocre, leach of a system and just exist."

I know I might sound a tinge arrogant, but many misunderstand confidence as arrogance. I am often confident to the point of scaring the people around me. However, I am never arrogant. I always know deep in my heart that anyone on earth can achieve anything they commit to. Achievement must be made a necessity, not a wish. Of course, there is massive effort involved. But anyone who negotiates the effort needed to win has no commitment to win and thus makes winning a wish—*period*. When one commits, effort is but an asterisk in the grand scheme of things.

I see three major ways to contribute. I know that everyone who works contributes to society in some form or another. However, I am talking about a higher level of contribution. One way is to serve in the military. The second way is to be a spiritual leader such as a pastor, rabbi, priest, pandit, or imam. The third way is to become financially successful, create jobs, and donate to legitimate charities. I chose the third way. I worked hard to become financially successful. I created jobs, and I give to my church and some select charities.

All who work for a living also contribute in a host of different ways. However, those contributions are pretty much a wash between self and community. For example, if you are working for a dry cleaner, you are certainly serving the community, but the contribution is a wash between what you do for the community and the money you earn for yourself.

A third thing happened at the end of 1979, completing the saying that things happen in threes. I was on one of my trips to Afghanistan in December and had checked into the Kabul Sheraton, my usual hotel of choice. One morning, I was shaving at around 5:00 a.m. local time when I heard a rumbling and felt the building reverberate. I wondered if we were in the midst of an earthquake or something. Suddenly there was a blast, and the Sheraton felt as if it were going to collapse.

DIVERSIFYING MORE

What actually happened was that Russian tanks driven by the rebels opposing President Daoud's regime were rolling into the city on the main thoroughfare, and one of the idiots opened fire and blew a massive hole in the hotel's coffee shop. I turned on the TV only to see a lot of propaganda. With the little I understood of Pashto, I pieced together that there was no earthquake and that we were in the midst of a coup d'état.

The rebels, backed by the Russians, had overpowered the broadcast facilities and the airport. The Russian-led coup was on in full force. I was just getting my head wrapped around what was going on when I was shaken by a pounding on my door. I gingerly looked through the peephole and saw a European guy, scared stiff and banging on my door. I opened it, and the guy rushed in without being invited. With a heavy French accent, he told me his name was Francoise and that he was a journalist. Nearly crying, he said, "I don't want to die." I told him to calm down and get hold of himself. I said, "If you are a journalist, shouldn't you be out there covering this huge story? It is by far the scoop of a lifetime. This could put you, a relatively unknown journalist, on the world stage overnight."

He was literally shaking with fear and told me that he wrote about ancient artifacts and antiquities. He said he was a nonviolent, passive human being. As grave as the whole situation was, I wanted to laugh. If it was me, I would have switched my journalistic genre from artifacts and antiquities in a New York minute and covered the freaking coup. My uncle was married to a woman from

HARD WORK AND THE AMERICAN DREAM

Cannes, the south of France. This wimpy guy reminded me of her—a lot of talk, tons of excuses, and no chutzpah.

Oh well. What do you want from a guy who grew up in France, a nation that gave up its sovereignty to Hitler without firing a shot? Their claim to fame was that they had the Resistance. Don't forget that France was the nation that dumped their colony (South Vietnam) into the hands of their NATO ally (America) when Vietnam's botched government got too hot to handle. They fled, and America was caught holding the bag. Ten years of honoring the treaty, and we realized the South Vietnamese were never willing to fight for their own freedom. They wanted the US to do it all for them. All of us alive at the time witnessed the civil unrest in the US that prompted President Richard Nixon (who was already being impeached and in political hot water) to pull out of the Vietnam War. The very moment the last helicopter was leaving Saigon, evacuating the final US Embassy personnel, the Viet Cong were rolling into Saigon.

France also gave safe haven to "Baby Doc" Duvalier from Haiti whose Ton-Ton Makoute, a vile group of trained killers, were responsible for hundreds of thousands of the deaths of their own people. France also gave safe haven to the Ayatollah Khomeini for years so that over time he could mount a successful coup against the Shah of Iran. We have a festering cancer that subsequently needs to be addressed now, due to France's failed policies and Jimmy Carter's inept strategy and passive behavior.

DIVERSIFYING MORE

My father was a senior military officer who fought and served during four wars in his 39 years of service. He said something extremely wise. "Son, don't pick a fight, ever. However, if they come at you, give 'em hell." The Iranians under Khomeini committed an act of war and came at the USA, yet President Carter did not give 'em hell. The results of his policies are plain to see. So I categorically say that in my eyes, France is not a good role model at all, and this wimpy French journalist was a true reflection of the country as a whole. I hate when incompetent people, organizations, and nations act superior and preach to the world about how things should be, while they are totally inept and incapable of doing what's right. The French have made an art form of ineptitude.

Well, back to the Afghan coup. My contractor, Mohamed, who ran the factory I owned with him, called and said, "Are you aware of what is going on? I am coming over immediately to pick you up. Hurry up and pack a light bag with essentials. We need to lie low for a while until things settle down. I need to get you out of the city. We'll go to a nearby village where I have friends and family. It will be safe."

I said, "I have a French reporter with me. We need to take him along as well."

"Is he going to be a problem?"

"He is scared stiff and almost in tears," I said. "We cannot leave him behind."

"Okay," he said.

I packed some toiletries and basics, underwear, socks, and some shirts, pants, and jacket. I told Francoise to do the same and hurry if he didn't want to be left behind. He was very happy I was taking him with me. Within half an hour, we were speeding out of the city of Kabul in Mohammed's very old but well-maintained car to a remote village about 90 minutes outside Kabul. We stayed there four days and listened to the radio all day for the news. We lived in huts made of clay and other rudimentary building materials (some bricks and stones) with a thatched roof. We slept on the floor and ate sitting under a tree near the village well with cats, dogs, chickens, goats, and cattle roaming around free. It was eye-opening to note that the animals were freer and less stressed than we humans were. After living in luxury in a penthouse in Boston and the Sheraton Hotel in Kabul, another amazing realization was how swiftly we humans can adapt to extremely rough and dire circumstances when compelled to do so. I just took it for what it was. If you believe in God, you don't complain or worry. You just count it all joy. I would have liked a hot shower with some good shampoo and body wash, though.

On the fifth day, early in the morning, we heard on the radio that things were under control and the airport was going to open. Pan Am was flying the first international flight out of Kabul to New Delhi that afternoon. I had a Pan Am ticket, so I told Mohammed I wanted to be on that flight. I asked Francoise if he wanted to get on the flight as well, but he said he did not have a Pan Am ticket. He had an Air France ticket. He said he would buy one and fly out with me. I asked, "What if you cannot get a Pan Am ticket? How will you fly out with me?"

DIVERSIFYING MORE

He said he would plead with the airlines, and if he could not fly out, he would just stay at the airport until he could. I told Mohamed we needed to leave right away. He said okay, and we left for the 90-minute ride about six hours before the flight was scheduled to leave. The drive was ho-hum for about an hour before we detected a rebel roadblock in the distance down the only road leading to the airport. We had no choice; we would have to go through it. The problem was that rabid, power-hungry men with primitive attitudes, no value for life, and no education were armed with Kalashnikovs. I didn't like that at all.

Mohamed talked to the driver in Pashto, but I got the gist of it. He told the driver to stop at the roadblock and let him handle the talking completely. He specifically told the driver not to say a word unless he was directly asked a question by the militia. He told me to relax and that he would introduce me as his Indian business partner. He would say Francoise was a tourist from France whom I had befriended. It was a fairly straightforward and believable scenario. The car came to a full halt, and three of the rebels came over, dressed in shalwars, long kurtas, long vests with sandals, and large lopsided turbans. They had terribly unkempt beards and carried automatic weapons pointed straight at us. One of them spoke in Pashto and asked where we were headed.

Mohamed answered in Pashto. "To the airport. My Indian brother and his French friend are leaving for New Delhi, India, on the Pan Am flight."

The rebel spokesman said, "Does the Indian speak Urdu?"

I answered *han* (yes) and smiled. He asked me if I was going to New Delhi. I answered in perfect Urdu with the right inflection and accent. *"Han mein Dilli ja raha hoon, apne matha aur pitha se milne"* (Yes, I am going to Delhi to visit my mother and father). He then swung his automatic weapon from left to right, implying that I was accepted as a local. Phew! I was relieved. It was pretty intense looking at the barrel of three Kalashnikovs trained directly at us. Then they asked about Francoise.

Mohamed said the foreigner was a French tourist I had met and befriended. The rebel asked me if that was true. I said, *"Han, mein use Kabul me mila"* (Yes, I met him in Kabul). He asked for his passport. At that point, Francoise was trembling and very fidgety. I told Francoise they wanted his passport, but he was nervous, thinking they would not give it back. I looked at Francoise sternly and said through clenched teeth, "Your passport." He gave it to me, and I handed it to the rebel who was doing all the talking. He opened it backwards because they wrote from right to left, and all their books and documents reflected that. I knew he could not make heads or tails of the passport. Again, although it was a very serious life-and-death situation, I suppressed the desire to laugh out loud. After what seemed like a considerable amount of scrutiny, he handed Francoise's passport to me and waved us on. Without another word said, the air was breathable again, and we were all relieved.

Unfortunately, on the outskirts of the Kabul International Airport, we encountered another checkpoint. This time, the guys were equally illiterate with automatic Kalashnikovs, but they were barking loudly and fiercely at us. They were far more aggressive and less trusting than the rebels at the previous checkpoint. It was harrowing, to say the least. The Frenchman did everything he could to keep from literally crying; he was such a wimp. I had to tell him several times to get hold of himself or we would all die right there. They kept conferring with the other militants at the checkpoint, and I thought we would be detained and miss the flight. Finally, after what seemed an eternity, they waved us on. Interestingly, they never asked me for my passport, I assumed because I had a beard, long hair, and resembled them. They took it that I was a brother from India. Little did they know that their assumed brother was carrying an American passport. I did not cater to their point of view at all and was the enemy by default.

We proceeded to the airport, and I asked Mohamed to stay in the car outside the airport and leave only after the Pan Am flight took off in case we didn't make the flight and needed to go back with him.

At the airport, it got really wacky. The rebels took over while the Russians stayed in the background so the coup could look authentically Afghan and not Russian. The Russian political stance was that they were helping the will of the people and not occupying another country.

Once inside the terminal, I proceeded to work on getting Francoise on the flight. Good news! Since we went there so early, we were able to snag a seat for

Francoise as well. After many hours, they called the flight in Pashto, but since there was only one flight leaving, everyone proceeded to the gate. We all had to fill out exit cards. However, the rebels who were in charge were illiterate or spoke only the vernacular—Pashto. They had done away with all who had any bureaucratic training whatsoever. To top it off, they definitely could not read or write English. I went up to the counter when it was my turn and handed the man my exit card. He looked at it seriously (he didn't understand a damn thing, and I knew it) and then turned it around, gave it back to me, and asked me to proceed. He never asked for my passport, and I never volunteered to show it to him. He waved me through the gate, and I pocketed the exit card he was supposed to keep for their records. What a farce! After what seemed to be an inordinate amount of time, armed militants came and allowed us to board the flight one at a time. We were relieved when the Pan Am staff took over after we entered the cabin. The head purser on Pan Am announced that we must not exhibit any exuberance and do things such as clap or show any excitement at all since it might be misconstrued for arrogance and jeopardize our departure.

Somberly, the plane filled. We were all relieved but remained quiet. Finally, the captain announced that the doors were closed and we were cleared for take-off, but celebrating was not allowed until we were not only airborne but also out of Afghan airspace. Then we sat on the tarmac about 90 minutes, which seemed like a year. At last, we started to taxi, and since we were the only flight, we got on the main runway in short order and took off.

People smiled at each other, but everyone kept totally silent. After a while, we saw the Kandahar Mountains, and I knew we were in good shape. Suddenly, the intercom crackled, and the pilot declared, "Ladies and gentlemen, we are free. We have crossed the Afghan border and are flying over Pakistan on our way to New Delhi." The applause was bigger and lasted longer than an encore for a Rolling Stones concert. I suddenly felt the intense pressure of the last five days literally leave my body. Francoise broke down and sobbed with tears of joy. He wore his emotions not on his sleeve but on his face. I was happy for him.

In a few hours, we landed in New Delhi. As I entered the terminal (there were no jetways; we had to take a bus after deplaning), a reporter from *Time* magazine shoved a microphone in my face and asked, "Sir, how do you feel now that you have made it safely out of Kabul?" I said, "Awesome," and before I could make a statement, he moved to another passenger. So I was misquoted as "an Indian passenger thought the coup in Afghanistan (where they killed the entire Daoud family, the youngest being a toddler) was awesome." I was so angry for being portrayed like that, even though they didn't name me. I felt awesome because I had made it through the ordeal, not because of the coup. I wanted to elaborate but was not given a chance to do so. The press can tell the truth and still promote fake news either by parsing words or aborting your answer before you frame your thoughts into a coherent sentence. My takeaway was this: Never trust the news.

The media loves to sensationalize everything, often with a political agenda that always favors their narrative. They use the power of the press to their ends. In the era of satellite TV, news rarely covers reality. The media often are distorters of the truth and downright liars.

My parents were relieved to see that I had made it out of Kabul. My girlfriend was also happy when I called her in the US and told her I was safe in New Delhi. A week later, things totally quieted down. Ariana Airlines (Afghanistan's flag carrier) resumed a daily flight from Delhi to Kabul and back. Against my parents' desire, I decided to fly back to Kabul to meet Mohamed and get my luggage and belongings from the Sheraton.

The stupidity started right at the New Delhi Airport. Ariana Airlines used a gate that did not belong to them. They had rebels deputized at the airport to handle the daily flight. They were dressed in civilian clothes posing as airline employees. The trained airline employees who knew how to handle airport protocols were probably sent back to Afghanistan and probably jailed or killed, considering they had belonged to the Daoud government. The rebels told all male passengers to form two lines and all female passengers to form two lines. Then the men were told to face each other, and the women were told to do the same. Once we did so, they barked at us, pointing a finger at the first person and saying, "You check you" and then switching the finger to the opposite person and saying, "You check you." Similarly, the women were instructed to do the same. So we passengers were the security check agents for each other. Many had to control themselves from bursting into laughter as we followed these ridiculous instructions. We boarded the plane none the worse for it all. I prayed the pilots were not rebel wackos. They were fine. We took off and landed without much fanfare.

I caught a taxi and asked the driver to take me to the Kabul Sheraton. As we were driving, we came to a T-junction with a sign that read POTS. I casually saw the sign, and we proceeded. We came to another intersection with another sign that read POTS. Then it hit me. Within a week, the illiterate rebels had changed all the traffic signs on the main arteries. Since they wrote from right to left, they changed the STOP signs to POTS signs. I laughed as I had never laughed before in that taxi in Kabul. The driver wanted to know what happened, but I just said, "I thought of something that was very funny" and didn't even try to explain it to him.

I checked into the hotel, and the front desk sent my luggage and other things I'd left up to my room. I tried to contact Mohammed, but his phone was dead. I then called the factory to see what we needed to do to get back on track with business, but the phone was disconnected. I took a cab to the factory, and the place was locked with no one in sight. A passerby told me that all property now belonged to the government. On the spot, I lost my factory and about a quarter of a million dollars. Who says foreign governments don't affect people's lives around the world? The cost of a war that neither I nor the country I belonged to was part of cost me a quarter of a million 1979 dollars. Today, that would be losing about $4 million dollars. For a small businessman, it was certainly a large amount of money as well as a huge loss of ongoing revenue due to the loss of my factory and the revenue and jobs it generated.

There are three basic ways to lose money when you are in business for yourself. Two of the three reasons have nothing to do with the person who is in business. The first is stupidity, making mistakes for one reason or another. The second is market conditions. And the third is government policies. Government policies could be war, regulations, taxes, interest rates, and on and on.

Chapter 27

SUCCESS IS SWEET REVENGE

In 1980, something stupendous happened. My restaurant Pondicherry located at 429 Boylston Street in Boston was named the number-one Indian restaurant in America by a leading food publication. Come to think of it, it was a foregone conclusion that it would have been voted the best because I hired the best of the best and brought them to the US to create what had definitely been the best Mughlai cuisine served in the USA. The saddest thing is that it has forever spoiled me. I have yet to eat Indian food that good anywhere else in the world, bar none. The food was never spicy hot; it was always made with an intricate blend of spices so complicated and subtle that the best of the best would find it hard to replicate. No matter what dish you ordered, you got a dance of flavor all over your palate, some as gentle as the foxtrot and others as outrageous as the tango. The food was always delicious beyond compare. When I was in NYC, I still frequented the Restaurant Rasoi now and then. On one of my trips, the owner came to my table and asked, "Who owns the Pondicherry restaurant in Boston that won the best Indian restaurant award? Have you eaten there? Is the food really that good?"

Smiling, I said, "You actually know the owner."

Confused, he said, "I do?"

I said, "Yes, I own the restaurant. Remember last November when I asked you to open a restaurant in Boston? You not only turned me down, you trashed the city of Boston as some hick town. My friend, you left me no choice but to open a restaurant and teach you a lesson."

He asked me, "Are you a chef?"

I said, "Buddy, if I was a chef, I would never have asked you to open a restaurant in Boston."

I was brought up with an attitude that enables me to think I can do anything, and I live that attitude. Not only did I open a restaurant, I opened an award-winning restaurant. Rasoi remained a very good restaurant, and I frequented it when I was in NYC. However, Pondicherry was the best Indian restaurant in the USA. I swear, success is such sweet revenge!

Life was downright exciting but hectic. Through it all, things were going well. Every day, major issues loomed up ahead, while other issues were being resolved. It was a nonstop affair of dealing with the good, the bad, and the ugly. Running four stores and owning a restaurant that was open to the public 12 hours every day 365 days a year was strenuous to say the least. I worked 14 to 16 hours a day at an exhausting pace. It was a nonstop combination of joy, stress, exhaustion, and passion. Through it all, I was simultaneously putting out fires every day. To some, it would be too much, and because of that, they would not deserve to even wish to live large. To me, it meant thriving every moment of every day and then going to bed feeling like I was truly accomplishing something meaningful. I was creating jobs. I was creating wealth. I was developing the opportunities that God opened up to me. I was thriving! I found out that the majority of people restrict themselves or acquiesce to others who restrict them from availing themselves of all that is out there. God loves it when you take on a task he has given you to accomplish and work hard. God loves it when we do justice to the amazingly capable mind and body he has given us. All we have to do is work and believe, and he accomplishes everything for us. He has equipped us with inordinate powers to overcome and succeed in anything our hearts desire.

One might say that evil often seems to have more success than good. That is so not true. Here are some glaring examples of it, one ancient and the others more contemporary. In the Old Testament, the evil Philistines used Goliath as their front man. Evil initially seemed to have more success than good did. However, ultimately, the Philistines were not just defeated; they were crushed. In modern times, Hitler and his Nazi regime were also evil. Again, evil seemed to initially have more success than good. However, Hitler (who was equally if not more evil than the Philistines) was ultimately not just defeated; he and his Nazi army were crushed. Pol Pot of Cambodia was another murderous heathen. He, too, seemed to be initially succeeding only to be crushed and die in exile a worthless, despised human being. Idi Amin, a despot from Uganda, seemed to be succeeding for years, again only to be crushed and exiled while dying as a worthless human being.

We must remember that Satan was once the most powerful archangel called Lucifer. He learned everything from God and decided to challenge God, the creator of the universe. He was exiled, but he has not been terminated yet for reasons God does not allow us to be privy to. Satan learned everything from God and remains a very powerful, evil being. He loves making people do evil things and portrays them as successful. That shakes the belief of the weak so they fall into his trap.

God gave us the Ten Commandments through Moses so we will live a good life. However, he never willed the Ten Commandments on us; he gave them to us. We have the free will to follow them or not, and boy, has humankind asserted its free will! There are good repercussions if we follow his Ten Commandments and bad repercussions if we don't. If we choose to sell out to God, we will not only thrive on earth and have the power to overcome all adversity while doing so, but when we die, we will qualify to exist in eternal bliss, spending the rest of eternity in heaven with the Almighty. If, on the other hand, we sell out to the devil, we can seemingly thrive on earth, but we will constantly suffer while having that temporary success and never attain eternal bliss, spending the rest of eternity in hell. I personally pick the former as my credo since I like success on earth, and I like having the power to overcome all adversity and reserve myself a place where there is eternal bliss—heaven!

www.ingramcontent.com/pod-product-compliance
Lightning Source LLC
Chambersburg PA
CBHW062157080426
42734CB00010B/1730